Medieval
Antisemitism?

PAST IMPERFECT

Past Imperfect presents concise critical overviews of the latest research by the world's leading scholars. Subjects cross the full range of fields in the period ca. 400—1500 CE which, in a European context, is known as the Middle Ages. Anyone interested in this period will be enthralled and enlightened by these overviews, written in provocative but accessible language. These affordable paperbacks prove that the era still retains a powerful resonance and impact throughout the world today.

Director and Editor-in-Chief

Simon Forde, *'s-Hertogenbosch*

Production

Ruth Kennedy, *Adelaide*

Medieval Antisemitism?

François Soyer

ARC HUMANITIES PRESS

British Library Cataloguing in Publication Data
A catalogue record for this book is available from the British Library

© **2019, Arc Humanities Press, Leeds**

ISBN (print): 9781641890076
e-ISBN (PDF): 9781641890083
e-ISBN (EPUB): 9781641890090

www.arc-humanities.org
Printed and bound by CPI Group (UK) Ltd, Croydon, CR0 4YY

Contents

Contents

List of Illustrations

Introduction

In October 2012, I was invited to give a research seminar paper on anti-Jewish propaganda produced in the late medieval and early modern Iberian world at an Australian university. The title of the paper included the term "antisemitic propaganda" and the terms "antisemitic" and "antisemitism" were used a few times during the paper. In the question and answer session that followed the paper, several academics in the audience—historians of twentieth-century Europe—vigorously questioned the appropriateness of using the concept of "antisemitism" in a pre-modern context. I was forcefully reminded that antisemitism is a "racial hatred of Jews," linked to the rise of "scientific racism" in the nineteenth century. Therefore, whilst "modern" hatred of Jews is racial, pre-modern hatred of Jews was distinguished and defined by its purely religious character. It was the height of absurdity, a terrible anachronism even, for a historian to use the concept of "antisemitism" in a medieval or early modern context.

Such a reaction will not come as a surprise to historians who have worked on the subject of anti-Jewish sentiment and propaganda in medieval Christian Europe. "Antisemitism" is certainly a nineteenth-century term that defies any facile attempt to define it. Kenneth L. Marcus has articulated the crux of the problem:

> To open up the question of the definition of anti-Semitism is to encounter one puzzle after another, each opening into the next like a set of Russian nesting dolls. To begin with, are

we defining an attitude, a form of conduct, or an ideology or pathology?[1]

In a twenty-first-century context, "antisemitism" has been used to define, alternatively, a refusal to recognize the legitimacy of the existence of a Jewish homeland (the State of Israel), criticism of Zionism as an ideology and movement, or indeed sometimes even criticism of Israeli government policies in Gaza and the West Bank. Some writers have even argued that these now constitute a "new" form of "antisemitism," adding another layer of complexity to the problem of defining "antisemitism." Even if it is reduced to its vaguest (and most imperfect) definition as "a hatred of Jews," the use of "antisemitism" is problematic. Does it merely mean a hatred of Jews defined as a specific racial/ethnic group? Can it, perhaps, be used more broadly to refer to the much-older refusal to accept or tolerate the existence of Jews as a separate or unassimilated religious minority, not just amongst medieval Christians but even earlier in pagan Antiquity?

In a short but thought-provoking blog post on the usage of the concept of antisemitism before the nineteenth century, Matt Chalmers has concluded that, whilst there are undeniable pros and cons for using the concept of "medieval antisemitism," "whether we want to use "antisemitism" or not, thinking about what is at stake in our choices can concentrate our attention on what we want to get out of the past."[2] The objective of this book is to argue that a simplistic division between a "medieval" Anti-Judaism supposedly distinguished by its religious nature and a "modern" antisemitism characterized by a racial focus is not helpful for historians. Without ignoring the important scientific, political, and socio-economic developments of the nineteenth and twenti-

---

1 Kenneth L. Marcus, *The Definition of Anti-Semitism* (Oxford: Oxford University Press, 2015), 30.

2 Matt Chalmers, *"Anti-Semitism" before "Semites": The Risks and Rewards of Anachronism* www.publicmedievalist.com/anti-semitism-before-semites/ [accessed August 23, 2017].

eth centuries that helped shape anti-Jewish ideology in the modern period, it is possible to make an argument in favour of "medieval antisemitism." This justification hangs not only on the importance of highlighting the elements of continuity between the "medieval" and the "modern" in anti-Jewish iconography and prejudice. Rather, it also hinges on a recognition of the importance played by the later Middle Ages as a period when significant numbers of Christian polemicists began to turn away from the Augustinian doctrine of grudging toleration of Jews as "living letters of the Law." Instead, Jews were often stripped of any individual identity by polemicists who presented them as a malignant collective with a hive mind, whose main objective was the destruction not only of the Christian faith but also of Christians themselves.

To achieve its purpose, the four chapters of this book focus on how anti-Jewish sentiment and propaganda in this period far exceeded the limits of pure religious dispute and polemic. The first chapter offers a historiographical survey of the use of the concept of "antisemitism" in a medieval context as well as the different ways that historians have justified their usage of the term and the controversies that this has consequently aroused. The following two chapters then focus on evolving Christian perceptions of the status of Jews in Christian society as well as the demonization and dehumanization of Jews from the twelfth century onwards.

In Chapter 2, we will be introduced to the formulation by St. Augustine in the early fifth century of what eventually became a doctrine of Christian toleration of Jews as a "witness people." We will then see how the Christian "discovery" of the Talmud in the twelfth and thirteenth centuries began to alter the attitude of some theologians and led them to question the status of Jews as a tolerable minority. The determining role played by the newly created Franciscan and Dominican orders in the thirteenth and fourteenth centuries is also analysed. Their missionary focus led them to examine and translate Talmudic writings and use these for their polemical purposes. As a result of these efforts, medieval Jews were increasingly perceived as perverted followers of the Talmud:

"Talmudists" whose anti-Christian rituals and presence could no longer be tolerated in a Christian-majority society.

In Chapter 3, the focus will be on how Jews came to be subjected to increased dehumanization and demonization in the writings of some Christian authors, popular folklore, and Christian iconography. This chapter will examine the transformation of the Jewish body into an object of caricature and disgust, the rise of the host desecration allegations and the Blood Libel as well as the emergence of conspiracy theories about a demonic "Jewish plot" to destroy Christendom.

Finally, the fourth and concluding chapter of this book will turn its attention to ominous developments in that part of medieval Christian Europe with the largest Jewish population: the Iberian Peninsula. A wave of mass (often forced) conversions from 1391 onward and suspicion of the religious sincerity of the converts and their descendants led to the appearance of what could be described as the first explicitly racialized form of "antisemitism" in which Judaism was presented as a biological trait, passed from generation to generation by those "infected" by the "Jewish blood" of their ancestors.

Chapter 1

Historians, "Medieval Antisemitism," and the Problem of Anachronism

Historical anachronism—the utilization or application by historians of concepts or key terms that did not exist in the period that they are studying—has long been held to constitute one of the cardinal sins that historians can commit. Accusations of historical anachronism have generated many debates amongst historians and the appropriateness of using the term "antisemitism" to refer to anti-Jewish rhetoric and sentiment expressed in the western world prior to the nineteenth century, and especially in the medieval period, is a salient example. Furthermore, the debate has been complicated considerably by the fact that there is no consensus about the definition of the term "antisemitism" itself or even whether the term should be spelled "antisemitism" or "anti-Semitism." Whilst "antisemitism" is commonly used as a generic shorthand for a hatred of Jews, such a definition is far too general to be used uncritically by historians seeking to examine the complexities of pre-modern Christian–Jewish relations. This chapter sets out to examine the different ways in which historians have used the term "antisemitism" in a medieval context since the late nineteenth century. The existing literature on the history of "antisemitism" and Christian–Jewish relations is vast and this chapter will present only a concise analysis of the heated controversies generated by the use of the term "antisemitism." As the concept of "race" is considered to be vital to any definition of "antisemitism," it then endeavours to survey the different perspectives of scholars (both historians and non-historians) on the existence of "race" in Europe during the Middle Ages.

It has been repeatedly and rightly pointed out that the term itself was apparently first used by the German journalist Wilhelm Marr (1819–1904), who founded the League of Antisemites (*Antisemiten-Liga*) in 1879, and it became popularized by Marr and others in the 1880s. Moreover, for many historians of antisemitism, the concept carries a clear racial component. Marr and other antisemites defined Jews collectively by their supposedly shared ethnicity and "racial identity" as "Semites" rather than their adherence to the religion of Judaism in order to distinguish them from "Aryans." The concept built on the theories of nineteenth-century anthropologists who conflated linguistics and ethnicity to produce "Semitic races" (thus racializing both Jews and Muslims as "Semites"). In the eyes of many modern antisemites, even conversion to Christianity does not turn a Jew into a Christian. As such, it does not seem possible to separate the concept of antisemitism from the rise of "scientific racism" and the racial theories that emerged in the nineteenth century. Given this historical context, the use of the terms antisemites and antisemitism in a medieval context might well appear highly contentious: at best an imprecise use of language or, at worst, a grave anachronism. If historians are supposed to formulate their arguments using only primary sources as their evidence, how can medievalists examining Christian–Jewish relations legitimately use terms and concepts that did not exist before the nineteenth century? Is the search for a causal relationship between the past and the present, linking the persecutions of the medieval period to the horrors of the Holocaust leading many historians into error?

One of the first historians to seriously consider the issue of the origins of modern antisemitism was the Frenchman Bernard Lazare (1865–1903), in his pioneering *L'Antisémitisme: Son histoire et ses causes* (1894). In Lazare's eyes, the gradual emancipation of European Jews after 1750 and the socio-economical upheavals and tensions that it generated created a new form of Jew-hatred. His analysis is worth quoting in full:

Anti-Judaism, which had been religious at first, became economic, or, rather, the religious causes, that had once been
dominant in anti-Judaism, were subordinated to economic
and social causes. This transformation, which corresponded
with the change in the [economic and social] role played by
the Jews, was not the only one. Once sentimental in nature,
the hostility towards the Jews became one of reason. The
Christians of yesteryear instinctively hated the deicides
and never attempted to justify their animosity: rather, they
showed it. The anti-Semites of today have conceived a
desire to explain their hatred and dignify it: anti-Judaism
was transformed into antisemitism.[1]

For Lazare, there thus existed a clear dividing line separating
the nineteenth-century antisemitism whose growth throughout Europe he was personally witnessing and the anti-Jewish
hatred of earlier centuries. It is interesting to note that Lazare
favours socio-economic factors over the rise of racial theories
in this analysis but his position is nonetheless crystal clear in
its implication: antisemitism did not exist before modernity
and Lazare evidently would not have understood the notion
of "medieval antisemitism," let alone acknowledged its historical validity.

Another historian influenced by contemporary events was
the Reform Rabbi Joshua Trachtenberg (1904–1959), the author
of the influential 1943 work *The Devil and the Jews: The Medieval Conception of the Jew and its Relation to Modern Antisemitism*. This work was written in the wake of the rise to power of
National-Socialism in Germany after 1933 and the persecution
of Jews that it unleashed, albeit before the full horror of the
Holocaust had been revealed to the world. For Rabbi Trachtenberg, unlike Lazare, there was a direct causal link between the
Jew-hatred of the medieval period and modern antisemitism.
This link was the literal demonization of Jews and their portrayal as bloodthirsty, inhuman monsters whose main concern was to destroy both Christianity and Christians.

I Bernard Lazare, *L'Antisémitisme. Son histoire et ses causes* (Paris:
Chailley, 1894), 222–45 at 227.

Trachtenberg concedes that hatred of Jews was far older than either the medieval period or even Christianity itself but contends that "its unique demonological character is of medieval origin [...] born of a combination of cultural and historical factors peculiar to Christian Europe in the later Middle Ages." The association of Jews with satanic black magic as well as with the perpetration of fantasized crimes such as the systematic desecration of consecrated hosts or the ritual murder of Christian children (the "Blood Libel") is therefore of crucial importance. There is also, in Trachtenberg's eyes, a geographical link between twentieth-century antisemitism and the "medieval conception of the Jew":

> Modern so-called "scientific" antisemitism is not an invention of Hitler's. But it was born in Germany during the last century, and it has flourished primarily in Central and Eastern Europe, where medieval ideas and conditions have persisted until this day, and where the medieval conception of the Jew which underlies the prevailing emotional antipathy toward him was and still is most deeply rooted.[2]

It is noteworthy that rather than explicitly using "medieval antisemitism" in his work, Trachtenberg prefers to distinguish "the medieval conception of the Jew" from "modern antisemitism." Trachtenberg does not explain why this is the case but it seems possible to infer from his work that his concern lay more in drawing the links between the medieval and modern conceptions of the Jew rather than debating the historical merits or dangers of adopting a specific terminology.

It is perhaps understandable that the issue of precise terminology came to seem less significant after the fall of the Third Reich in 1945 laid bare the horrific mass murder of millions of Jews during the Holocaust. French historian of the Holocaust Léon Poliakov (1910–1997) authored an impressive five volume *Histoire de l'antisémitisme*, originally published

---

2 Joshua Trachtenberg, *The Devil and the Jews: The Medieval Conception of the Jew and its Relation to Modern Anti-Semitism* (Philadelphia: Jewish Publication Society, 1993), 4–5.

between 1955 and 1994. In the earlier volumes of his opus, published during the 1950s and 1960s, Poliakov made no bones about employing the concept of antisemitism to refer to anti-Jewish thought and sentiment from Antiquity (and the very earliest history of Christianity) to the modern era and, unsurprisingly, applying it to the medieval period as well. This broad usage of the term does not, however, belie the fact that Poliakov was aware of the evolution and differences in anti-Jewish sentiment across this vast expanse of time. Another noted historian of modern European Jewry, Jacob Katz, essentially followed the same line in his seminal work *From Prejudice to Destruction: Anti-Semitism, 1700-1933*, published by Harvard University Press in 1980. Katz notes at the very beginning of his book (page v) that "Prejudice against Jews—anti-Semitism in modern parlance—has been strangely persistent since its first appearance in ancient times."

Since the 1980s, historians of Christian–Jewish relations in the Middle Ages have, of course, continued to grapple with this historical problem. Their efforts have yielded new approaches and new controversies. The single most important advance was made by Gavin Langmuir (1924–2005) in his aptly entitled book *Toward a Definition of Antisemitism* (1990). In this pioneering exploration of medieval anti-Jewish sentiment and rhetoric, Langmuir supported the view that antisemitism can indeed be traced as far back as the medieval period in Christendom and he went even further, claiming that it actually has its origins in medieval Europe:

> If by "antisemitism" we mean not only its racist manifestations but all instances in which people, because they are labelled Jews, are feared as symbols of subhumanity and hated for threatening characteristics they do not in fact possess, then antisemitism in all but name was widespread in northern Europe by 1350, when many believed that Jews were beings incapable of fully rational thought who conspired to overthrow Christendom, who committed ritual crucifixions, ritual cannibalism, and host desecration, and who caused the Black Death by poisoning wells—even though no one had observed Jews committing any of those crimes.

> Unknown to the ancient world, antisemitism emerged in the Middle Ages, along with so many other features of later Western culture. It is one contribution to which historians of the majority cannot point with pride, so most medievalists have avoided discussing it until very recently.[3]

For Langmuir, the medieval period was characterized, from the large-scale massacre of Jews at the beginning of the First Crusade in 1096 onward, by a transformation in Christian attitudes towards Jews.

It is important to emphasize that Langmuir's argument was not reduced to arguing that there existed a rift between, on one hand, an anti-Judaism which resulted in the coexistence of a "rational" religiously motivated anti-Judaism, in which the Jew was hated as the adherent of a rival, competing, religion, and, on the other hand, an "irrational" antisemitism, in which the Jew was hated and feared as a demonic agent and accused of appalling crimes such as the ritual murder of children or the poisoning of wells. Instead of formulating a simplistic definition, Langmuir provides the following definitions of anti-Judaism and antisemitism:

- Anti-Judaism is a non-rational hostility to Jews or Judaism that is based on characteristics that Jews actually possess (which is not to say that the hostility itself is justified).

- Antisemitism can be defined as a hostility to Jews that is based on characteristics that Jews do not possess. Moreover, there is no empirical evidence that would form the basis for thinking that Jews actually do possess these characteristics.

The rationale for these definitions lies in Langmuir's contention that all religious beliefs are inherently non-rational because they are neither rational (supported by purely empirical evidence) nor irrational (contrary to rational thought).

---

3 Gavin Langmuir, *Toward a Definition of Antisemitism* (Berkeley: University of California Press, 1990), 301–2.

"antisemitism" (or its adjectival form "antisemitic"), it follows, is a term that can legitimately be used when referring to demonstrably false Christian beliefs about the Jews. These beliefs, which Langmuir describes as "chimerical," include the false and unprovable notion that Jews ritually murdered children in accordance with Talmudic precepts or that they had horns/tails.[4]

Langmuir's definition would appear, on the surface, to be a perfectly simple and reasonable one but it has nonetheless failed to satisfy many historians. Numerous historians have expressed uneasiness that the use of "antisemitism" risks muddying the waters by obscuring the differences that existed between pre- and post-nineteenth-century anti-Jewish thought. The German historian Johannes Heil has sounded a note of caution, noting that terms are "bearers of meaning" (*Bedeutungsträger*) and has argued forcefully in favour of using the terms "Anti-Judaism" or "Judeophobia" rather than "antisemitism" for the pre-modern period.[5] Many German historians have been able to skirt the issue of terminology by employing the term *Judenhass* ("Jew-hatred") instead. Likewise, wary of comparisons with the modern era, Anna Sapir Abulafia has taken issue with Langmuir's point of view, preferring to employ "anti-Judaism" rather than "antisemitism," arguing that it is important not to "obscure" the complexity of medieval Christian attitudes towards Jews.[6]

The most sophisticated critique of Langmuir's concept of "medieval antisemitism" has been produced by another historian specializing in medieval European Jewry: the eminent scholar, and professor of Hebrew & Judaic studies, Robert

4 Langmuir elaborated this concept in his two seminal works *History, Religion, and Antisemitism* (Berkeley: University of California Press, 1990), 275–305 and *Toward a Definition of Antisemitism*.

5 Johannes Heil, "'Antijudaismus' und 'Antisemitismus': Begriffe als Bedeutungsträger," *Jahrbuch für Antisemitismusforschung* (1997): 92–114.

6 Anna Sapir Abulafia, *Christians and Jews in the Twelfth-Century Renaissance* (London: Routledge, 2005), 4–7.

Chazan. In Chazan's opinion, Langmuir's use of the notions of "rational," "non-rational," and "irrational" to help forge the concept of "medieval antisemitism" and distinguish it from "anti-Judaism" are highly problematic from a methodological perspective. Langmuir's decision to employ such a concept is flawed by the way that it "ultimately distorts our everyday use of the word irrational" and does not note the metaphorical dimension of many anti-Jewish claims. Moreover, Chazan points to a major flaw in Langmuir's definition of antisemitism: that it is not entirely satisfactory from a factual point of view. Indeed, as we shall see in Chapter 3 of this book, the Blood Libel allegations were investigated, demonstrated to be patently false, and unambiguously denounced in the medieval period by both the Papacy and many secular Christian authorities.

Chazan's objections are not limited to points of methodology. They also extend to the risks of creating a wider distortion of the history of anti-Jewish thought and feeling. The misuse of terminology, he argues, presents a grave risk for historians as it neglects the "gradations" in anti-Jewish feeling:

> Not surprisingly, those charged with responsibility for safeguarding Jewish interests in the post-World War II world are loathe to assign gradations to manifestations of anti-Jewish feeling or action. Yet the refusal to allow for such gradations in its turn bears unacceptable results. Particularly in a post-Holocaust setting, it seems crucial to maintain some sense of the truly horrific nature of the genocidal efforts of the Nazis. To transform every instance of social tension into an antisemitic event is ultimately to cheapen language that ought to conjure up unimaginable horror.

Chazan regrets that there is no concept in the English language that could adequately translate the Hebrew concept of *sin'at Yisrael* (שנאת ישראל), literally "a hatred of Israel" in which the notion of a hatred of both the religion of Judaism and of the Jewish people is coalesced.[7]

---

7 Robert Chazan, *Medieval Stereotypes and Modern Antisemitism* (Berkeley: University of California Press, 1997), 125–34.

Those seeking to distinguish between a medieval religious "anti-Judaism" and a modern "secular antisemitism" have also pointed to the intellectual and political effects of the Enlightenment in Europe. In his 1998 *Paths to Genocide: Antisemitism in Western History*, Lionel Steiman sought to explore the roots of modern antisemitism and pointed to the role played by "the philosophers who undermined the theological foundations of Jew-hatred [and who] replaced them with a more durable material." For Steiman, it was the "interrelated forces" of Jewish emancipation, rising national awareness (and the emergence of nationalism) as well as racial theories that gave rise to a distinct form of Jew-hatred revolving around the "Jewish Question" in modern Europe.[8]

Despite such clearly divergent positions, many modern historians have adopted a pragmatic usage of the concept of "antisemitism" in a medieval context even when they either explicitly express scepticism about it or acknowledge that its use is problematic. The historian Robert Stacey, for instance, claims that "to speak of medieval English antisemitism is to risk both anachronism and obloquy. It can be argued [...] that the term, especially with its overtones of late nineteenth-century 'scientific racialism,' has no place in a medieval context." Nevertheless, Stacy concedes that Gavin Langmuir's explanation, although controversial, is compelling and that the use of the concept of a "medieval antisemitism" seems justified. More recently, Rebecca Rist has elected to resort to the expedient of using both Anti-Judaism and antisemitism in her work to distinguish polemical attacks on the religion of Judaism from the polemical and physical attacks on "the Jewish people as a race."[9] Whilst such a pragmatic approach is commend-

---

8 Lionel B. Steiman, *Paths to Genocide: Antisemitism in Western History* (New York: St. Martin's, 1998), xiii.

9 Robert C. Stacey "Anti-Semitism and the Medieval English State," in *The Medieval State: Essays Presented to James Campbell*, ed. J. R. Maddicott and D. M. Palliser (London: Hambledon, 2000), 163–77, and Rebecca Rist, *Popes and Jews, 1095–1291* (Oxford: Oxford University Press, 2016), xiii.

able in its rejection of the simplistic categorization of medieval anti-Jewish thoughts as either "anti-Judaism" or "antisemitism," it does little to help clarify a confusing situation.

Given the significance that many historians have often attached to the racialized aspects of "modern" antisemitism, there has not been much attempt to study anti-Jewish thought in the Middle Ages alongside the putative existence of proto-racial ideas in the same period. Gavin Langmuir's search for a definition of "medieval antisemitism" certainly did lead him to consider "racism" and "ethnic prejudice" as potential elements but he rejected both of these as too problematic. To include "race" in the definition was deemed to be unhelpful by Langmuir since, he believed, this risked implicitly validating the nineteenth-century racial theories that had led Wilhelm Marr and others to propagate fantasies about the "Aryan" and "Semitic" races as well as the concept of "antisemitism" after the 1870s. Moreover, whether in a medieval or modern context, "race" was to be eschewed since "contemporary biologists no longer believe there are distinct racial boundaries between humans, only differences in the relative commonness of certain hereditary traits."[10]

If "race" is therefore a flawed concept in Langmuir's eyes, that of "ethnic prejudice" is only slightly less so. Langmuir notes that its origins are, admittedly, to be found in the theories of social scientists regarding hostility between different human groups rather than "the rationalizations of racists or the presuppositions of the victims of such hostility." This advantage, however, is negated by various problems. Firstly, it results in a perceived tendency amongst social scientists to adopt theories and definitions of "ethnic prejudice" that are "too inclusive" and with a marked tendency towards faulty generalization. Even though its exceptional longevity and intensity is often noted, antisemitic prejudice is thus largely equated with other forms of "ethnic prejudice," such as white prejudice against blacks or prejudice between different European peoples. This approach does not take into account the

---

10 Langmuir, *Toward a Definition of Antisemitism*, 311–13.

specificities that characterize Christian–Jewish relations and fails to differentiate it from these other forms of prejudice.[11]

Concerns about using the concept of "race" in a medieval context must, of course, be discussed in relation to the existing medieval terminology. Langmuir's fear of "trivializing" anti-Jewish sentiment by making it just one form of cultural bigotry amongst others probably explains why little attempt has been made to examine side by side the historical appropriateness of using "antisemitism" or "race" in historical contexts pre-dating the nineteenth century. Despite Langmuir's scepticism, this is crucial in the light of recent historiographical developments. The concept of "race" (and therefore by extension of "racism") has recently become the subject of a parallel debate over the anachronism of using this concept in reference to the Middle Ages. Many scholars now argue that the notion that "race" is a purely modern construct needs to be challenged as simplistic or, at the very least, nuanced considerably. Robert Bartlett in particular has noted the significance of the vocabulary that we can find in medieval sources: "some of the key terms of medieval Latin usage, such as *gens* and *natio*, imply, etymologically, a concept of races as descent groups." This descent or lineage is often traced back to a biblical or legendary figure but for Bartlett there can be no doubt that the medieval concept of ethnicity transcended simple biology, coalescing it with culture:

> An even sharper contrast with a primordial biological view of race is found in the common emphasis that medieval authors placed on the cultural component of ethnic identity. For the majority of medieval writers, ethnicity was defined by and manifested in culture as much as, or more than, descent. The classic and much-quoted definition of Regino of Prüm (d. 915) asserts that "the various nations differ in descent, customs, language and law" [*diversae nationes populorum inter se discrepant genere, moribus, lingua, legibus*]. Of the four criteria listed here, only one is biological.[12]

11 Langmuir, *Toward a Definition of Antisemitism*, 316–17.

12 R. Bartlett, "Medieval and Modern Concepts of Race and Ethni-

Even though it might appear odd to a modern reader accustomed to thinking of racial categorizations in exclusively "biological" terms, this mixing of heredity, culture, language, and religion to define a *gens* or *natio* reflects the complexity of the medieval world.

The translation of *gens* as "race" rather than the more neutral "people" remains controversial but it is supported by an increasing body of scholarship. Even though Bartlett's discussion focuses particularly on the different Christian peoples of the British Isles (the English, Scots, and Welsh) and medieval Europe, and mentions Jews only tangentially, it is certainly the case that there are many references in medieval texts from across Europe to the Jews as representing a *gens Iudaeorum*, *populum iudaicum*, or *gens hebraeorum* in their own right, a usage of *gens* that might well have been encouraged by the presence of such concepts in the Vulgate Bible (Esther 3:7 and I Maccabees 8:20–25 and 12:3–13:42). The notion of a *gens Iudaeorum* that tied medieval Jews to their biblical forebears, thereby carries the same mixture of biological and cultural–religious connotations that the use of *gens* has when used in reference to other peoples. Interestingly, it is also possible to find similar references to Muslims as a *gens Sarracenorum* or *gens Ismaelitarum*, linking them to a biblical origin story as descendants of Ishmael.[13]

Whilst the somewhat fluid Latin terms *gens* and *natio* were commonly used, especially in Northern Europe, the Romance word from which English derived "race"—French (*race*), Italian (*razza*), and Castilian (Spanish, *raza*)—did exist in southern Europe and were no invention of the nineteenth century. Its etymology—whether it is derived from the French *haras* (the word for a stud farm) or from the Arabic *ra's* (indicating "origin" or "head")—is still the object of debate. Certainly, as the

---

13 On the usage of *gens* and other proto-racial terms in medieval Europe see Paul B. Sturtevant in www.publicmedievalist.com/medieval-people-racist/ [accessed February 14, 2019].

French scholar Charles de Miramon has noted, the term "race" appears in the late Middle Ages usually in the context of horse or dog breeding and discussions regarding the pedigree of such animals. Yet Miramon sounds a note of caution about linking the usage of "race" to humans in the medieval period:

> The dominant medieval discourse leaves little room for a concept of race or human sub-species [...]. The medieval prehistory of "race" models the cultural matrix that was to witness the growth of the uses of race and hereditary blood in the second half of the sixteenth century.

Given its use in animal husbandry, it was perhaps inevitable that use of the term was very occasionally extended to denote differences due to genealogical descent amongst humans. The examples of this are rare but mostly come from the Iberian Peninsula and are related to aristocratic pedigree. Such a usage of the term *raza* in relation to humans can be found in Castilian (Spanish) as early as 1438 in a satirical work entitled *El Corbacho: Reprobación del amor mundano*. The author, Alfonso Martínez de Toledo, distinguishes aristocratic men of "good race" (*buena raza*) from those of "vile race and lineage" (*vil raza y linaje*) whose behaviour and interests would always be influenced by their lowborn genealogy. Even in the first half of the sixteenth century, the term "race" was not preferred when discussing Jews. The rejection of an applicant seeking to study in the Spanish college of San Clemente in the University of Bologna (Italy) in 1530 contrasted his "very aristocratic *raza*" on one side of his family tree with the lamentable "Jewish lineage" (*estirpe hebrea*) of the other.[14]

Such a narrow focus on the terminology used to convey notions of ethnicity and heredity in the medieval period risks losing sight of the wider issues. The celebrated historian of race and racism George Fredrickson has expanded the argument of Joshua Trachtenberg and argued in favour of a "reli-

---

14 Baltasar Cuart Moner, *Colegiales mayores y limpieza de sangre durante la Edad Moderna* (Salamanca: Ediciones Universidad de Salamanca, 1991), 62.

gious racism or racialized religiosity" in which Jews and Muslims were effectively dehumanized and demonized through an association with the Devil and his evil works. For George Fredrickson, racism is closely tied to the actions of individuals and institutions rather than to precise terminology or the existence of racial theories:

> Racism, as I conceive it, is not merely an attitude or set of beliefs; it also expresses itself in the practices, institutions, and structures that a sense of deep difference justifies and validates. Racism, therefore, is more than theorizing about human differences or thinking badly of a group over which one has no control. It either directly sustains or proposes to establish a racial order, a permanent group hierarchy that is believed to reflect the laws of nature or the decrees of God. [...] Anti-Judaism became antisemitism whenever it turned into a consuming hatred that made getting rid of the Jews seem preferable to trying to convert them, and antisemitism became racism when the belief took hold that Jews were intrinsically and organically evil.[15]

Most recently, Francisco Bethencourt has authored an impressively exhaustive analysis of documentary evidence ranging across the medieval and modern periods and has opined that "racism" ("prejudices concerning ethnic descent coupled with discriminatory action") in the West clearly preceded the modern theories of "race." Moreover, he argues convincingly that "racism" must not be understood as a monolithic modern construct but rather as a phenomenon with different and independent historical meanings: in essence we should not hesitate to talk about the historical existence of various forms of "racisms" (plural) rather than "racism" (singular).[16]

Modern scholars of medieval studies working with critical race theory and postmodernism in the English and Philosophy

---

15 George Fredrickson, *Racism: A Short History* (Princeton: Princeton University Press, 2002), 6 and 19.

16 Francisco Bethencourt, *Racisms: From the Crusades to the Twentieth Century* (Princeton: Princeton University Press, 2014).

departments of universities have also insisted that we need to reframe the concept of "race" in the medieval period. Jeffrey Jerome Cohen, for instance, posits that "race" "is identity lodged in the body, no matter how specious" whilst "ethnicity," on the other hand, is "identity as expressed in culture." Such scholars note that there is no single or stable meaning of "race" and that it has flexible definitions in which it can intersect with gender, class, or sexuality. When it comes to Jews in medieval England, Geraldine Heng and Dorothy Kim have argued that the use of "race" is justified because it is centred on, and linked to, the body. Segregationist legislation and decrees, such as those promulgated by the papacy in the early thirteenth century, expressed anxieties about the physical similarly of Jews (and Muslims) and, correspondingly, sought to create and impose a visible physical barrier between religious groups. Likewise, they both highlight the significance of caricatures and libels relating to physical aspects of the Jew's body (such as grotesquely crooked noses or a particular bodily odour).[17] Consequently, "racial" (somatic or bodily) factors are just as crucial as cultural factors when it comes to understanding the way that non-Christian and non-white peoples were "othered" in medieval Europe.

Prior to concluding, it is important to highlight the fact that the significance of the historical debate over the use of the term "antisemitism" in the medieval period is one that extends beyond academic monographs or conferences. It is a historical debate that bears directly on modern Christian–Jewish relations and the need of all modern Christians (not just Catholics) to consider the history of their faith and how its

---

17 For the critical theory and postmodernist perspective see Geraldine Heng, "The Invention of Race in the European Middle Ages I: Race Studies, Modernity, and the Middle Ages" and "The Invention of Race in the European Middle Ages II: Locations of Medieval Race," *Literature Compass* 8, no. 5 (May 2011): 258–74 and 275–93. Also Dorothy Kim, "Reframing Race and Jewish/Christian Relations in the Middle Ages," *Transversal: Journal for Jewish Studies* 13 (2015): 52–64.

treatment and perception of Jews in its medieval past relates to modern horrors. Indeed, an insistence on a stark distinction between medieval "anti-Judaism" and modern "antisemitism" can easily lead to an unconscious or conscious distortion of history. At worst, this approach can even be used to serve the interests of apologists and propagandists.

During the papacy of John Paul II (1978–2005), the Vatican commissioned a report into the responsibility of the Catholic Church and Pope Pius XII (1939–1958) in the Holocaust. The report, which was completed in 1998, presented the argument that modern antisemitism is defined by the view that the Jews are a separate and inferior race. Since, the report concludes, the Catholic Church always opposed and condemned racial discrimination it cannot be held responsible for modern antisemitism. Nonetheless, as David Kertzer has persuasively argued in his research on the papacy's role in modern antisemitism, this is an argument with many logical problems. It reduces modern antisemitism to a single component, racism, whilst ignoring its other facets:

> The logical problem in the Vatican argument then comes down to this: if the Church bore major (though of course not exclusive) responsibility for the inculcation of a dozen of the major ideological pillars of the modern antisemitic movement, but a thirteenth came from other sources, are we to conclude that the Church bears little or no responsibility for the flowering of modern antisemitism in those areas where the Church had great influence?[18]

Moreover, as Kertzer has claimed and this book will argue in the following chapters, neither is it the case that the Church can be exculpated from the creation of a proto-racialized conception of Jews during the medieval period.

---

18 David Kertzer, *The Popes against the Jews. The Vatican's Role in the Rise of Modern Anti-Semitism* (New York: Knopf, 2001), 205–6 at 206.

Conclusion

It would be easy to be disheartened by the inability of historians (and scholars in other academic disciplines) to agree on the historical validity of using the concepts of "antisemitism" and "race" in the medieval period. This book does not seek to examine the "origins" of antisemitism. Instead, it argues that a simple opposition between a "modern" racialized antisemitism and a "medieval" religious anti-Judaism makes little sense in light of the fact that anti-Jewish attitudes in medieval Europe were multifaceted. These attitudes evolved into new forms in the centuries between ca. 1100 and 1500, they varied across different parts of Europe and even among the individuals expressing them.

The historicity of using the concept of antisemitism in a medieval context therefore needs to be re-evaluated in much the same way as the use of the concept of race. As we shall see in the following chapters, medieval rabbinical Judaism came to be characterized by some Christian theologians not just as a rival faith whose followers needed to be converted to Christianity but as a post-biblical religious movement with little legitimacy and in some cases even as a cannibalistic death cult thirsting for Christian blood. Moreover, proto-racialized ideas about Jews did exist and some thinkers promoted a hatred of Jews that essentialized their faith and culture to the point where these became the functional equivalent of race. This book argues that we need to talk about different antisemitisms (plural) rather than a single antisemitism (singular) and that there is a case to be made that "medieval antisemitism" can be a historically useful concept that can be used without the fear of anachronistically mapping modern notions of race onto a medieval context.

Chapter 2

Judaism and the Jews in Medieval European Religious Thought

In the first three centuries after the crucifixion of Christ, the relationship of the early church with Jews was dominated by anxieties about the identity of Christianity as a separate religious movement whose faithful included Gentiles as well as Jews. The debate between the Apostles Paul and Peter over circumcision and the decision to abandon compulsory circumcision "in the flesh" (the Old Covenant) did not abate worries that Jews would influence early Christians to "judaize." This chapter, however, focuses on the perception of the Jew in Christian thought *after* Christianity became the dominant religious movement in the Mediterranean Basin and Western Europe. Its focus is on thinkers in Western (Roman Catholic) Christendom from the fifth century to the close of the fifteenth century.

What status should Jews, who refuse to accept Christ's Messiahship, have in a majority Christian society? This question exercised the minds and drained the inkwells of numerous Christian theologians throughout the medieval period. As it will become clear in this chapter, the work of St. Augustine in the early fifth century helped to establish a theological framework for a form of grudging religious pluralism in which Jews had a place in Christian society. The Augustinian concept of the Jews as a "witness people" to be tolerated proved to be enduring and became the guiding policy of the papacy. From the twelfth and thirteenth centuries onward, however, many theologians were influenced by the works of Jewish converts to Christianity and their "revelations" about the Talmud and rabbinical Judaism. The result was a distinct hardening of attitudes towards Jews and, in some cases, a renewed questioning of their status in Christian society. Just as significantly, the rise of a polemical Christian tradition that focused on the Talmud was to have very serious consequences for Christian–Jewish relations in the modern era.

St. Augustine's "Witness People"

The first Christian theologian to formulate a clear status for Jews in a majority Christian society was the prolific theologian St. Augustine, bishop of Hippo in North Africa (354–430). To understand Augustine's doctrine regarding the Jews, it is important to remember the historical context in which the bishop was writing. Christianity had become a tolerated religion in the Roman Empire since the edict of Milan in 313, but it had only become the official faith of the empire since the Edict of Thessalonica in 380. Paganism remained widespread after 380 as did divergent ("heretical") forms of Christianity (such as Donatism, Manichaeism, or Arianism). Moreover, the spread of Nicene Christianity was seemingly jeopardized by the crumbling of the western half of the Roman Empire and the arrival of Germanic tribes who not only usurped imperial authority in the west but also embraced Arian Christianity. Augustine himself would die (of natural causes) in a Carthage under siege by the Arian Vandals.[1]

The place of Judaism and Jews in a Christian Roman Empire was unclear after 380. For many Christians, Jews were not only the followers of a faith rendered obsolete by the triumph of Christianity but dangerous as it risked perverting the faith of Christians. Early Christian polemicists such as Tertullian (ca. 155–ca. 240) and John Chrysostom (ca. 349–407)

---

1 For a detailed analysis of Augustine's position on the Jews see Paula Fredricksen, *Augustine and the Jews: A Christian Defense of Jews and Judaism* (New Haven: Yale University Press), 2008.

had already attacked Judaism and the threat presented by "judaizing Christians." Bishop Ambrose of Milan wrote to the emperor in 388 to defend Christians who had burned a synagogue in Syria. His letter, however, went further by advocating the persecution of Jews and the curtailment of Jewish religious freedoms. The destruction of synagogues, described as sites of demon-worship, by Christian mobs was nothing less than a manifestation of God's will for the Bishop of Milan. In 414 St. Cyril, the Bishop of Alexandria, expelled the Jews from Alexandria and in 417–418 the well-established Jewish community of the Balearic island Minorca was converted under threat of violence and its synagogue was destroyed.

It is in this volatile context that Augustine approached the problem of the Jews' status in Christendom. Augustine's attitude to the Jews was shaped by his refutation of the heretical movement of Manicheism, which rejected the validity of the Old Testament. Himself a Manichean until his conversion to the Catholic Church in 386, Augustine defended the Old Testament in his work *Contra Faustum* (ca. 399) by pointing to the Jews as witnesses of its validity. Later, his views on the status of the Jews were clearly articulated in his great work *City of God*, written after 410, in a chapter entitled "Of the Birth of Our Saviour, Whereby the Word Was Made Flesh; And of the Dispersion of the Jews Among All Nations, as Had Been Prophesied" (bk. 18, chap. 46):

> God has thus shown to the Church the grace of his mercy in the case of her enemies the Jews, since, as the Apostle says, "their failure means salvation for the Gentiles." And this is the reason for his forbearing to slay them—that is for not putting an end to their existence as Jews, although they have been conquered by the Romans; it is for fear that they should forget the Law of God and thus fail to bear convincing witness on the point I am now dealing with. Thus it was not enough for the Psalmist to say, "Do not slay them, lest at some time they forget your Law," without adding, "Scatter them." For if they lived that testimony of the Scriptures only in their own land, and not everywhere, the obvious result would be that the Church, which is everywhere, would

not have them available among all nations as witnesses to the prophecies which were given beforehand concerning Christ.[2]

For Augustine, Psalm 59:11 was crucial to understanding the significance of the continued existence of Jewish communities centuries after life of Christ. The Jews are the "witness people" because

- Against the claims of Manicheans, the Jews witness that the Old Testament, which prefigures Christ, is true.

- By their miserable status as exiles dispersed in the Mediterranean diaspora after the Roman destruction of Jerusalem in 70, the Jews continue to bear witness that Jesus truly is the Messiah to all the Gentile Christians.

- Finally, the Jews bear the "mark of Cain." Like Cain, they are protected by God and are allowed to live (i.e., continue in their Jewish worship).

Significantly, Augustine was not writing about the Jews who were his contemporaries in the early fifth century. Instead, the Jews to whom Augustine referred were essentially relegated to the status of "fossils" (as a number of modern historians have put it), relics of Antiquity and the Old Testament. Their continued existence was necessary to convince any wavering Christians of the truth of Christ's existence and the validity of his claim to be the Messiah. Augustine's apparent defense of the Jews was certainly not motivated by feelings of empathy for the Jews or sympathy for their plight. Augustine's intention was therefore essentially to justify the validity of the Old Testament and never to establish a doctrine about the status of Jews in Christian society.

It is important not to oversimplify the later reception of Augustine's concept of the Jews as a "witness people." Other early medieval Catholic theologians who turned their atten-

---

2 Augustine of Hippo, *City of God*, trans. Henry Bettenson and ed. G. R. Evans (London: Penguin, 2003), 828.

tion to the Jews, such as Gregory the Great (ca. 540–604) and Isidore of Seville (ca. 560–636), accepted the premise of the Jews' status as witnesses to the validity of Christianity but still advocated active measures to convert them to Christianity. Nevertheless, Augustine's writings about the Jews are significant because of their widespread dissemination in the monastery and university libraries of medieval Europe. The papal bull *Sicut Iudaeis*, first issued in the twelfth century and then periodically re-issued during the later medieval period, threatened excommunication against Christians who physically attacked Jews, sought to force them to convert, damaged or stole their property, and interfered with their religious rites. This protection only held, however, so long as the Jews themselves did not seek "in their synagogues to exceed the limits placed upon them by the law." As such, the papal bull does not engage in outlining a theologically sanctioned status for Jews beyond one of a practical toleration.[3]

The Augustinian position was articulated far more explicitly when attacks on Jewish communities broke out prior to the start of the Second Crusade in 1147–1149. Abbot (and later St.) Bernard of Clairvaux, one of the principal preachers and promoters of the crusade, condemned the Christian rioters and prohibited others from persecuting Jews by appealing to the same biblical passage as Augustine:

> The Jews are not to be persecuted, killed, or even put to flight. Ask those who know the Sacred Scriptures what they read foretold of the Jews in the psalm. "God," says the Church, "instructs me concerning my enemies, 'slay them not, so that my people should not forget.'" The Jews are indeed for us the living letters of Scripture, constantly representing the Lord's Passion. They have been dispersed all over the world for this reason: so that in enduring just pun-

3 Jeremy Cohen, *Living Letters of the Law: Ideas of the Jew in Medieval Christianity* (Berkeley: University of California Press, 1999), 73–12; *The Apostolic See and the Jews*, vol. 1, *Documents: 492–1404*, edited by S. Simonsohn (Toronto: Pontifical Institute of Mediaeval Studies), 51–52.

ishments for such a crime wherever they are, they may be the witnesses of our redemption. Hence the Church, speaking in the same psalm, adds, "only disperse them in thy power, and subjugate them, God my protector." And so it has been done: dispersed and subjugated they are: under Christian princes they endure a harsh captivity. But "they will be converted toward the end of time," and "it will be at the time of their redemption."[4]

For St. Bernard, the Jews were by a biblical injunction mere "living letters"/"living words" (*vivi apices*) of Scripture. A living reminder to all Christians of the Passion of Christ and whose miserable remnants were dispersed throughout the world by God's divine will to fulfil this task. Moreover, their acceptance as a minority in Christian society was justified by the fact that they would play a crucial role heralding the Apocalypse and Second Coming of the Messiah by their mass conversion.[5]

Another famous and influential clergyman of the midtwelfth century, the Abbot of Cluny Peter the Venerable, also followed Augustine's reading of Psalm 59:11 in a letter directed to King Louis VII of France before his departure on crusade. Peter, however, could not hide his utter contempt for the Jews, who are rated as worse than Muslims:

But what value in pursuing and attacking the enemies of the Christian faith in remote and distant lands, while the Jews, wretched blasphemers far worse than the Saracens, not far away from us but in our midst so freely and audaciously blaspheme, abuse, and trample on Christ and the Christian sacraments with impunity?[6]

Peter was nonetheless clear that the reason Jews must be tolerated was that it was God's will that the Jews "be preserved for a life worse than death," condemned to wander

---

4 Cohen, *Living Letters of the Law*, 235–36.

5 Cohen, *Living Letters of the Law*, 242.

6 Chazan, *Medieval Stereotypes and Modern Antisemitism*, 49.

the earth like Cain and suffer ignominy for spilling the blood of Christ until their eventual conversion and the Second Coming of the Messiah.

In the first decade of the thirteenth century, the Augustinian position on Jews was reaffirmed by none other than Pope Innocent III (1198–1216), the most formidable medieval pontiff and an implacable opponent of those whom he perceived as a threat to Christendom. The attitude of Innocent III towards the Jewish minority in Christendom was ambivalent. In letters addressed to French bishops in 1205 and 1208, Innocent reasserted that Jews had, like Cain, been condemned by God "as a result of their own guilt" to wander over the earth, to suffer ignominy as well as "perpetual servitude" but he noted that they must not be killed "lest the Christian people forget the divine law." He was nevertheless greatly concerned that the rising economic influence of Jews as moneylenders would lead to a subversion of their acceptable socially inferior position in Christian society. In the Lateran Council of 1215, Innocent and the Church promulgated a ban on "excessively oppressive" Jewish usury as well as segregationist measures, most notably the wearing of distinctive symbols by Jews, to limit their social interactions with Christians and prevent any interfaith sexual relationships. Whilst it is tempting to interpret the actions of the papacy as representing a deliberate "policy of degradation" of the Jews, this would be too simplistic. In fact, the actions of the Holy See were primarily motivated by a concern for the spiritual welfare and unity of Christian society and the Christian faithful. The strict segregation and limitation of the socio-economic power of religious minorities (not just Jews but also Muslims) was, in papal eyes, a necessary corollary of such concerns and a prerequisite to their continued toleration. The immensely influential Dominican theologian Thomas Aquinas (1225–1274) followed the papal position and Augustinian doctrine on the Jews in his works, including the *Summa theologiae*. Finally, when the papacy established the Inquisition to root out heresy from Christendom, it was made clear that the Jews were not to be classed as heretics and therefore did not fall under the jurisdiction of inquisitorial tribunals.[7]

The Christian "Discovery" of the Talmud: From Tolerable "Witness People" to Intolerable "Talmudists"

The *Talmud*—a word that can be translated into English as "learning" or "instruction"—is a compendium of writings (sixty-three tractates) on Jewish law and religion. It contains both a compilation of oral Jewish law and the analyses and commentaries of rabbis. In the twelfth century, Christian polemicists began to use the Talmud as a source of information, which they claimed undermined the Jewish refusal to recognize Christ's identity as the Messiah. What can be termed as the Christian "discovery" of the Talmud was a gradual process. Although Innocent III does not mention the Talmud in his letters and decrees, Christian polemicists had first become aware of its significance a century before. The consequences of this "discovery" have been both long lasting and devastating for Jewish-Christian relations.

It would wrong to believe that Christian theologians has been completely unaware of rabbinical writings before the twelfth and thirteenth centuries. In late Antiquity, both St. Jerome (the translator of the Bible into Latin) and St. Augustine had been aware of Jewish oral traditions. They refer to the Mishnah, Jewish oral traditions written down in the first two centuries CE, and thus the earliest component of the Talmud, as the *deuterosis* (from the Greek δευτερωσις for "doubling"). In a commentary on Hosea 3:1, Jerome compared the Jews to an adulterous woman for spurning God's love and loving "useless things, the traditions of men, and their *deuterosis* fantasies." Likewise, St. Augustine noted in one of his works that the Jews possessed memorized but unwritten scriptures, "which they call *deuterosis*," in addition to the Old Testament. The Byzantine Emperor Justinian had prohibited Jews from publicly using

---

7 Rist, *Popes and Jews*, esp. 3–6.

their *deuterosis* to comment on the Old Testament in 553 and all Jewish converts to Christianity in post-Roman Visigothic Spain were likewise instructed in 637 to surrender their nonbiblical texts. In the early medieval period, however, the few Christian polemicists who attacked Judaism overlooked the Talmud.[8]

In 1106, the Jewish personal physician of the King of Aragón in Spain converted to Christianity. The convert was not only a talented medical practitioner but also a learned rabbi and astronomer named Moses who took the name Peter Alfonso (*Petrus Alfonsi*) in honour of his royal patron and godfather king Alfonso I. After his conversion, Peter Alfonso wrote a treatise entitled *Dialogus contra iudaeos* (Dialogue against the Jews) in which he staged a fictional debate between a Jew named Moses and a Christian named Peter: his former Jewish and present Christian selves. In the dialogue, the zealous neophyte made use of his extensive knowledge of postbiblical rabbinical scholarship. Peter accused rabbis of using the Talmud to mislead the Jews and to close their minds to the manifest veracity of Christian claims. In the prologue of his dialogue, Peter Alfonso dismisses the Talmud ("your teachings") as ridiculous nonsense:

> Are you not mindful of your teachers who wrote your teachings, on which your entire law relies, according to you [...]. And how they have advanced such opinions concerning [God] which appear to be nothing other than the words of little boys making jokes in school, or women telling old wives' tales in the streets.[9]

---

8 St Augustine, *Exposition on the Psalms*, Psalm 119: https://web.archive.org/web/20190131120835/https://faculty.gordon.edu/hu/bi/ted_hildebrandt/otesources/19-psalms/text/books/augustine-psalms/augustine-psalms.pdf [accessed January 31, 2019] and St. Jerome: https://web.archive.org/web/20190131121850/https://books.google.com.au/books?id=jHzYAAAAMAAJ&pg=PT349&redir_esc=y#v=onepage&q&f=false [accessed January 31, 2019].

9 Petrus Alfonsi, *Dialogue Against the Jews*, ed. and trans. Irven M. Resnick (Washington, DC: Catholic University of America Press, 2006), 46.

Using the legends and parables of the Talmud—the *Aggadot*—to condemn and disparage their authors as either insane, idiotic, or at the very least in error, Peter offered his readers a rational defence of Christianity and an attack on Judaism, which he presented as an irrational faith. In its systematic use of the Talmud, the work marks the starting point of a new trend in Christian polemical attacks on Judaism as a faith and, eventually, upon the Jews as a people. Moreover, his innovative polemic rapidly became popular in Western Europe and a source of inspiration for his successors and emulators.

During the 1140s, Abbot Peter the Venerable of Cluny, wrote a polemical treatise in Latin entitled *Adversus Judeorum inveteram duritiem* (Against the Inveterate Obduracy of the Jews). The objective of this work was to convince the Jews of the truth of Christ's claim to be the Messiah. Even though the work addresses the Jews, it was in fact evidently intended to provide Christian clergymen with the polemical tools that they would need to use when preaching to Jews and engaging in debates with rabbis. Peter's polemical text stands out, however, because his polemical strategy did not solely seek to find evidence favourable to Christianity in the Old Testament. In addition to this, Peter also sought to undermine the beliefs of the Jews by ridiculing the Talmud. Peter was the first Christian writer known to have referred to the Talmud by that name and to seek to use it as a source of polemical material. The entire fifth chapter of the work is dedicated to this purpose and entitled "On the Ridiculous and Very Foolish Fables of the Jews." Frustratingly, Peter does not reveal the source of his newfound knowledge of the Talmud, ascribing it to an almost divine revelation from God:

> I lead, then, the monstrous beast out from its lair, and push it laughing onto the stage of the whole world, in the view of all peoples. I display that book of yours to you in the presence of all, O Jew, O wild beast, that book, I say, that is your Talmud, that egregious teaching of yours that you prefer to the books of the prophets and to all authentic judgements. But do you wonder, since I am not a Jew, how this name became known to me; [...] who revealed to me the

Jewish secrets; who laid bare your intimate and most hidden secrets? It is he, he, I say, the Christ whom you deny.[10]

For the Abbot of Cluny the Talmud is a "ruinous text," a source of "insanity" that has "tainted" its Jewish readers with its impurities. Within Peter's polemic there thus resides a paradox. On the one hand, the Jews were rational agents who could be open to conversion through proper biblical exegesis and rational Christian argumentation. On the other hand, however, the Jews' attachment to the Talmud caused them to suffer from an irrational spiritual blindness.

Why was this development significant? The shift in the focus of Christian polemical writings on Jews and Judaism to include attacks on the Talmud and Rabbinical Judaism paved the way for a range of new anti-Jewish accusations. In the central Middles Ages, Christian polemicists and scholars in both northern and southern Europe, keen to convert Jews, increasingly pointed to bowdlerized passages from the Talmud in order to ridicule Rabbinic Judaism and thus "demonstrate" its supposedly manifest falseness and the veracity of Christ's claim to be the Messiah.

The creation of the Mendicant Orders—the Franciscans and Dominicans—in the early thirteenth centuries led to a surge of interest in the active evangelization of non-Christians: not just pagans or Muslims living beyond the political borders of Christendom but also amongst Jews and Muslims living under the authority of Christian princes. This missionary effort was aided by the active participation of an increasing number of zealous Jewish converts to Christianity. Amongst these neophytes was the Jewish convert and Franciscan Nicholas Donin, a former Jew expelled from the Jewish community in Paris who presented a list of thirty-five accusations against the Talmud to Pope Gregory IX in 1236. Donin accused the Jews of the kingdom of France of claiming that, beyond the

---

10 Peter the Venerable, *Against the Inveterate Obduracy of the Jews*, ed. and trans. Irven M. Resnick (Washington, DC: Catholic University of America Press, 2013), 212.

Ten Commandments handed down to Moses, "God gave them another Law, which is called the Talmud, that is 'teachings.' They lie that it was handed down to Moses orally and implanted in their minds." It was the rabbis, Donin asserted, who had written it down so that the Jews should not forget it and the result was that the Talmud contained "wicked and abusive things." Donin's arguments persuaded the Pope to order all Christian princes to confiscate copies of the Talmud in early 1240, although his decree was only implemented in the kingdom of France.[11]

The Christian polemicists and converts of the thirteenth century did not limit themselves to ridiculing Judaism. They also pointed to passages presented as blasphemous against Jesus Christ. These polemical attacks on the Talmud led to the great 1240 Disputation of Paris and the burning of twenty-four cartloads of copies of the Talmud in Paris in 1242. During the infamous "disputation" between Nicholas Donin and four French rabbis, which was in fact nothing less than a trial of the Talmud, the focus remained on the perceived anti-Christian blasphemies of the Talmud but another, darker new development occurred. To prove his point, Donin took a Talmudic dictum ("the best of Gentiles is to be killed") out of its context as part of a study of the book of Exodus and the Egyptian persecution to claim that the Talmud not only permitted but also encouraged the killing of Gentiles. Donin turned the dictum into a specifically anti-Christian one by substituting "Christians" for "Gentiles" (*optimum Christianorum occide*).[12]

In the years immediately following the Talmud burnings in Paris, it was Pope Gregory IX's successor, Innocent IV, who personally led the charge against the Talmud. Pope Innocent ordered his legate Odo of Châteauroux and various high-rank-

---

11 Cohen, *Living Letters of the Law*, 319–21.

12 *The Trial of the Talmud*, ed. John Friedman, Jean Connell Hoff, and Robert Chazan (Toronto: Pontifical Institute of Mediaeval Studies, 2012), 108–9.

ing churchmen to conduct an investigation into the Talmud. The legate's report in 1248 was unambiguous: the Talmud was "full of innumerable errors, abuses, blasphemies, and wickedness [...] and horrify the hearer to such an extent that these books cannot be tolerated in the name of God without injury to the Christian faith." The legate, unsurprisingly, recommended the seizure of all copies of the Talmud. Notwithstanding Odo's findings, the papacy had already begun to alter its position in 1247. Having considered a Jewish appeal against the measures taken in Paris, Innocent IV did not act upon the findings of his legate. Pope Innocent limited himself to ordering the return of copies of the Talmud to Jews after they had been expurgated of select passages deemed blasphemous. In 1264, Pope Clement IV ordered a renewed campaign of expurgation in eastern Spain but forbade any action against the Talmud that would violate the privileges which the papacy has conferred upon the Jews. For the remainder of the medieval period, the papacy did not proceed beyond periodic campaigns of expurgation.[13]

The Paris Disputation of 1240 was only the first of a number of such one-sided confrontations in which Christian polemicists forced rabbis to refute their arguments in favour of Christianity as well as their claims of Talmudic blasphemy. Further south, in Barcelona, a similar disputation was organized in 1263 between a convert to Christianity and Dominican friar named Paul Christian and the celebrated rabbi and philosopher Moses Nahmanides. In 1272, Paul Christian was present at a second disputation held in Paris. In Spain, another very similar disputation was organized in 1413–1414 in the town of Tortosa between rabbis and another convert and ex-rabbi named Jerónimo de Santa Fe, the author of works entitled *Contra perfidiam Judæorum* (Against the Perfidy of the Jews) and *De iudaicis erroribus ex Talmut* (The errors of the Jews according to the Talmud).

13 *The Trial of the Talmud*, ed. Friedman et al., 16–55; Cohen, *Living Letters of the Law*, 317–54.

Jewish converts to Christianity thus played a leading role in the growing awareness of the existence of the Talmud and its potential as a source of polemical ammunition. The push to evangelize Jews and Muslims also spurred a greater interest in the study of Hebrew and Arabic as the Dominican friar (and later saint) Raymond of Penyafort (ca. 1175–1275) established a *studium* or school for the study of these languages in Spain. Evidence of the resulting transformation of the Jews in Christian eyes can be easily discerned in one of the most notorious and influential anti-Jewish polemics of the medieval period, written by one of Penyafort's disciples. The *Pugio fidei adversus Mauros et Iudaeos* (Dagger of the Faith against Muslims and Jews) was completed in 1278 by the Dominican friar Raymond Martin (ca. 1220–1284). Friar Martin was not just a contemporary of Paul Christian but also one of his colleagues. Despite the title of the book, its principal target is rabbinical Judaism and the Jews. Citing passages from the Talmud in Hebrew or Aramaic and then providing Latin translations, Martin set out to prove that the coming of Christ the Messiah was not only foretold in the Old Testament but even in the Talmud and other rabbinic writings since, even though most rabbinic writing was fabrication, it still contained biblical roots.[14]

The most important aspect of the work of Raymond Martin, however, is his clear differentiation between the biblical "Old Jews" (*Iudaei antiqui*) of the Old Testament and the "modern" (i.e., medieval) Jews (*Iudaei moderni* or *Iudaei nostri temporis*). In Friar Martin's eyes, the "modern Jews" constitute a real threat to the Church and Christians. Their rabbinical writings corrupt the Old Testament and the rabbis thus connive to prevent the Jews from acknowledging the truth of the New Testament and Christ's claim to be Messiah. A passionate hatred of Christians consumes the "modern Jews" and they are more than willing to act out their hatred. According to Fray Martin, "[the Jews'] plan for Christians is this one:

---

14 Jeremy Cohen, *The Friars and the Jews: The Evolution of Medieval Anti-Judaism* (Ithaca: Cornell University Press, 1982), 129–38.

to kill Christians, and kill their children by casting them into wells and pits, when they can do this secretly."[15]

Raymond Martin and his work influenced many of the anti-Jewish polemics written from the second half of the thirteenth century onwards. Nicholas of Lyra (ca. 1270-1349), a French Franciscan who was a theologian more interested in biblical exegesis than active missionary work, followed the same line of distinguishing the biblical Jews from their medieval descendants. For Lyra, the obduracy of the Jews and their "spiritual blindness," was not the result of a divine curse but rather was primarily caused by the Jews' own free will and their unyielding attachment to the Talmud and "to their teachers' [i.e., the rabbis'] errors." In his biblical commentary on Jeremiah 13:23 ("Can the Ethiopian change his skin, or the leopard his spots? then may ye also do good, that are accustomed to do evil"), Lyra discussed the possibility of genuine Jewish conversions to Christianity and expressed considerable pessimism. The Prophet Jeremiah, he claims, spoke thus about the Jews who could not "revert to good because of their inclination to evil, and this inclination is their particular nature." For Lyra the genuine conversion to Christianity of a Jew, who is evil by nature, was unlikely without the intervention of God.[16]

By the fifteenth century, the notion that the Talmud was a force for evil that turned Jews into inveterate enemies of Christians had become firmly implanted in western Christendom. The convert Jerónimo de Santa Fe, for instance, ends his 1412 work *Contra Iudaeos* with chapters warning Christians that the Talmud corrupts Jews and "explicitly orders Jews to inflict all the harm that they can upon other peoples, especially Christians." This "harm" is supposedly not to be achieved just through frauds and thefts but also extends to physical violence. Like Donin over a century and a half before, Jerónimo de Santa Fe emphasizes the significance of the Talmudic dictum ("the best of Gentiles is to be killed") without

---

15 Cohen, *The Friars and the Jews*, 129-69.

16 Cohen, *The Friars and the Jews*, 170-95.

offering any explanatory context and expressly asserts that this meant "the best of the Christians."[17]

The most violent excoriation of the Talmud and attack upon Jews was that written around 1458–1464 by a Spanish Franciscan, Alonso de Espina with the prolix title: *Fortalitium fidei contra iudeos, saracenos aliosque christiane fidei inimicos* (Fortress of Faith against Jews, Saracens and all other enemies of the Christian faith). Espina's book was eventually printed in numerous editions in northern Europe from the end of the fifteenth century onward and became widely cited by authors in early modern Europe. The *Fortalitium fidei* is written in Latin but it is primarily a work of popular propaganda with Espina himself stating that the work was intended "for the ignorant" (*pro ignorantibus*). Even though there is a particular Spanish context for this work, which is analysed in Chapter 4, Espina's work fits into the pattern of increasing focus on the Talmud and the perceived visceral hatred that Jews harbour against Christians. The Franciscan mocks the Jews' failure to accept Christ's message and miracles, their obdurate devotion to the "Talmudic doctrine" (*talmudica doctrina*) and the observable "stupidities of the Jews" (*iudaeorum fatuitatibus*) which it allegedly contains.[18]

Espina, however, expounded opinions that went beyond those of his predecessors in terms of their vitriolic savagery and heartily embraced all manner of anti-Jewish conspiracy theories. The result was a narrative of Christian victimhood as Espina devoted a significant part of his polemic to enumerating and describing the "cruelties" that Jews inflicted upon Christians. This becomes a horrifying list of acts of treason in favour of Muslims, acts of ritual murder of Christian children,

---

17 Jerónimo de Santa Fe, *Contra Iudaeos Hieronymi de Sancta Fide, iudaei, ad christianismum conuersi. Libri duo: Quorum prior fidem & religionem eorum impugnat. Alter uero Talmuth* (Zürich: Geßner & Wyssenbach, 1552), 166–96.

18 Rosa Vidal Doval, *Misera Hispania: Jews and Conversos in Alonso de Espina's Fortalitium Fidei* (Oxford: Society for the Study of Medieval Languages and Literature, 2013).

the practice of black magic to plot the murder of innocent Christians, the poisoning of wells, and murders committed by Jewish doctors. For Espina, there can be no possible doubt that if the Jews represent an existential threat to all Christians it is because of the Talmud. Like Lyra, whom he references and quotes, Espina considers the possibility of sincere conversions to Christianity as extremely remote. God's intervention and "great virtue in the heart is necessary" for Jews, "who have been fed that [Jewish/Talmudic] doctrine since childhood" to accept the Christian faith.[19]

If the Jews were so dangerous because of their supposedly fanatical adherence to the Talmud, why should they be allowed to live amongst Christians? Even the harshest theologians and critics of the Talmud did not advocate the violent slaughter of the Jews living under Christian rule. Neither could they completely refute the possibility of sincere conversions to Christianity, although many saw such conversions as exceptional and the result of divine intervention. Moreover, in accordance with Scripture (Isaiah 10:22 and Romans 9:27), they accepted that the mass conversion of the Jews would herald Christ's second coming and that, until then, the Jews must be carefully reduced to the position of socially inferior outcasts.

Those who saw the Jews as too much of a threat to Christianity and Christians advocated two solutions that did not amount to physical mass murder: forced conversion or exile. The expulsions of Jews from England and France were mostly the result of secular rulers seeking to rid themselves of their financial obligations to Jewish moneylenders and to seize Jewish assets. They were usually justified as the result of excessive Jewish usury and were not directly influenced by the discourses of theologians. Nevertheless, some medieval theologians came to formulate justifications for the forced

---

19 François Soyer, "'All one in Christ Jesus'? Spiritual Closeness, Genealogical Determinism and the Conversion of Jews in Alonso de Espina's *Fortalitium Fidei*," *Journal of Spanish Cultural Studies* 17, no. 3 (2016): 239–54.

conversion or even forcible removal of Jews from Christian society. The Spanish missionary and polemicist Raymund Lull (1232–1316) argued in his work that Jewish men should be trained in Latin, philosophy and logic so that Christians may debate with them on equal term and, he assumed, convert them (and their families) to Christianity. Lull argued that any Jews who remained obdurate after such an education must no longer be tolerated and must be banished from Christendom. More drastically, the theologian and philosopher Duns Scotus (ca. 1266–1308), who was not an anti-Jewish polemicist and practically never mentioned Jews in his work, affirmed that forced conversions of Jews could be considered to constitute a legitimate part of a ruler's moral obligations. In his view, Romans 9:27 did not mean that all the Jews must be tolerated. For Duns Scotus, the forced baptism of Jews, especially children, "by threats and by striking terror" were a legitimate measure that would not contravene Romans 9:27 if a small reserve of Jews was allowed to subsist on an isolated island. Nearly two centuries later, the most extreme of all medieval polemicists, Alonso de Espina approvingly discussed the expulsions of the Jews from England and France. He saw then as an example that needed to be followed in the Iberian Peninsula and he also noted Duns Scotus's opinion that it was only necessary to preserve a few Jews on "some island." Expulsion did not represent a contradiction to Psalm 59:11 since it was not tantamount to extermination. Jews would be allowed to live, just not in Christian society.[20]

Conclusion: The Medieval Origin of the *Talmudjude*

The attitudes of medieval Christian theologians towards Jews in Western Christendom were thus far from straightforward.

---

20 Nancy L. Turner, "Jewish Witness, Forced Conversion, and Island Living: John Duns Scotus on Jews and Judaism," in *Christian Attitudes toward the Jews in the Twelfth and Thirteenth Centuries: A Casebook*, ed. Michael Frassetto (London: Routledge, 2007), 183–209.

Whilst many accepted the Augustinian concept of the Jews as a contemptible "witness people" to be tolerated, others increasingly saw Judaism and its faithful as a dangerous post-biblical sect. The logical progression of the arguments of men like Nicholas Donin, Paul Christian and Raymond Martin was that the link between the Jews of the Old Testament and the "modern Jews" had been decisively broken by the Talmud and rabbinical Judaism. Medieval Judaism was not Biblical Juda-ism but rather a Jewish heresy that threatened Christianity just like all other forms of heresy. The resulting image of the Jewish "other" was a terrifying one. Their minds warped by their rabbis' fanatical adherence to the Talmud, the Jews not only sought to ridicule Christianity through ritual blasphemy or acts of sacrilege but were also encouraged to rob and kill ordinary Christians, especially children.

This was a toxic seed that became firmly implanted in the most extreme anti-Jewish discourse and which prospered in the early modern period across Protestant and Catholic Europe. The increasing numbers of Jewish converts to Christi-anity as well as a growing interest in the study of Hebrew led to an ever-increasing focus on the Talmud by Christian polem-icists. The works of medieval polemicists, especially Lyra, influenced Martin Luther's notorious *On the Jews and their Lies* (1543) and his claim that "their Talmud and their rabbis record that it is no sin for a Jew to kill a Gentile" or to commit fraud against Gentiles.[21] The increasing focus that medieval theologians brought to bear on the Talmud established a last-ing pattern in Christian polemical writings. Modern authors followed the same path including Johannes Eisenmenger, the author of an influential encyclopaedic two-volume work *Ent-decktes Judenthum* (Judaism Revealed) printed in 1700, and the Catholic priest, Justinas Pranaitis, who published his noto-rious *The Talmud Unmasked (The Secret Rabbinical Teachings Concerning Christians)* in 1892.

---

21 Martin Luther, "On the Jews and their Lies," in *Luther's Works, Volume 47: The Christian in Society IV*, ed. H. T. Lehman and F. Sherman (Philadelphia: Fortress, 1971), 226.

Far from disappearing or being replaced by racial theories, Christian denunciations of the Talmud and rabbinical Judaism continued to represent an important part of anti-Jewish discourse in the nineteenth and twentieth centuries. The polemicist August Rohling published his influential *Der Talmudjude* (Münster, 1871) and in 1892 the quasi-official Vatican newspaper *L'Osservatore Romano* endorsed the claim that Jews committed ritual murder "in obedience to the Talmud." Even in Nazi Germany, racial prejudice against Jews was supplemented by attacks on the Talmud. Ironically, Alfred Rosenberg, one of the architects of Nazi racial theory and a great critic of Christianity, published *Unmoral im Talmud* (Immorality in the Talmud) in 1920 and the work was reprinted number of times between 1933 and 1943. Likewise, the 1938 Nazi picture book for children, *Der Giftpilz*, warned its young readers through rhyme that "in the Talmud it is written/ What Jews hate and what they love/ What Jews think and how they live/ All is ordained by the Talmud" (see Figure 1).[22]

---

22 Ernst Hiemer, *Der Giftpilz* (Nuremberg: Stürmer, 1939), 16–20 at 20.

„Im Talmud steht geschrieben: ,Nur der Jude allein ist Mensch. Die nichtjüdischen
Völker werden nicht Menschen genannt, sie werden als Vieh bezeichnet.' Und weil
wir Juden den Nichtjuden als Vieh betrachten, sagen wir zu ihm nur Goi."

Figure 1. Ernst Hiemer, *Der Giftpilz* (Nuremberg: Stürmer, 1939), 16.
What is in the Talmud? "In the Talmud it is written: "Only the Jew is
human. Gentile peoples are not called humans, but animals."
Since we Jews see gentiles as animals, we call them only Goy."

Chapter 3

The Dehumanization and Demonization of the Medieval Jews

The previous chapter has examined developments in how medieval Christian theologians perceived Judaism and the Jews. This chapter departs from the discourses of theologians on the status of Jews to focus on the evolving perception of the Jews in medieval Christian society more generally. The Christian notion of a relationship between the Jews and the Devil and of a perpetual curse afflicting Jews and distinguishing them from Gentiles has its origins firmly in the New Testament, namely Matthew 27:24–25 ("His blood is on us and on our children") and John 8:44 ("You belong to your father, the devil"). The medieval period witnessed what Joshua Trachtenberg accurately described in 1943 as a normalization of the representation of the Jew as an "alien, evil, antisocial, and anti-human creature, essentially subhuman," a demonic Jew who "was born of a combination of cultural and historical factors peculiar to Christian Europe in the later Middle Ages."[1]

The rise of an anti-Jewish discourse that demonized Jews in western Christendom occurred gradually and at the same time as Jewish communities were expanding not just in terms of their demographic and geographical distribution but also in terms of their economic significance. Jewish merchants and their families seeking economic opportunities migrated northwards from the Mediterranean area and established themselves across France, Germany, and (after the Norman

---

[1] Trachtenberg, *The Devil and the Jews*, 6.

Conquest in 1066) England. The expanding economy and urban centres of medieval western Europe as well as the Church's prohibition on Christians lending money at interest encouraged Jewish migration and involvement in moneylending and tax farming. It also encouraged Christians to perceive usury and Jewish economic activity as synonymous, entrenching an image of Jews in Christian eyes as parasitical and rapacious moneylenders.[2]

This chapter assesses the way in which Jews were dehumanized and demonized in medieval Europe. It departs from the theological discussions in the treatises and polemics of the previous chapter to focus on what could be described as "popular" anti-Jewish beliefs, prejudices, and stereotypes in the medieval period. The use of the term "popular" is employed to denote various ideas and concepts about Jews that were not officially endorsed by the medieval papacy but which were expressed in popular folklore, medieval iconography, or the writings of some churchmen. As such, this chapter explores four key topics. Firstly, it examines Christian perceptions of the Jewish body as an object of disgust and contempt. Secondly, it analyses the claims of systematic Jewish violence in the form of attacks on Christianity in deliberate acts of religious sacrilege. Thirdly, it will focus on the assertion that Jews also physically attacked Christians through the ritual murder of Christian children. Fourthly, it concludes by providing an insight into the evolving concept of a collective Jewish conspiracy against Christendom.

Constructing the "Jewish Body" as an Object of Disgust

One of the most enduring characteristics of modern antisemitic iconography has been the portrayal of Jews as physically, and therefore visually, different from Gentiles. It certainly

---

2 See chaps. 3, 4, and 5 of Robert Chazan, *The Jews of Medieval Western Christendom, 1000–1500* (Cambridge: Cambridge University Press, 2006).

seems that no nineteenth or twentieth-century antisemitic newspaper article, book, poster, or movie was complete without a grotesquely caricatured representation of the "Jew." The origins of the modern caricatures of the Jew can be found in stereotypes and images created during the medieval period, although it is difficult to know whether they originated in popular folklore, the writings of churchmen, or a merging of both of these. What is clear, however, is that the emergence of a distinctly "Jewish" physiognomy and body in anti-Jewish Christian writings and iconography stripped Jews of their individuality and therefore of their humanity. Collectively, the Jews became a physically repulsive and disgust-inducing "other."

The iconographic representation of Jews with grotesquely elongated noses only appeared gradually in the later medieval period. The recent research of Sarah Lipton has noted the absence of antisemitic iconography in depictions of Jews until the thirteenth century. Indeed, according to Lipton, the first explicitly anti-Jewish caricature can be dated to 1233 and appears in a doodle in the upper margin of an English exchequer tax receipt. The 1233 caricature, contained in an official document, which only a handful of royal officials in England would have seen, is clearly not the origin of this iconographical trend, whose precise origins remain obscure.[3] Jews with caricatured noses certainly start to appear in manuscript illumination produced across Western Christendom with increasing frequency from the end of the thirteenth century onwards from Spain to Germany. By way of illustration, illuminations in the *Cantigas de Santa Maria*, a compendium of poems from the court of King Alfonso X of Castile in the second half of the thirteenth century, feature Jewish men who can be distinguished from Christians by their prominent crooked/broken noses. In the illuminated English book

---

3 Sara Lipton, *Dark Mirror: The Medieval Origins of Anti-Jewish Iconography* (New York: Metropolitan, 2014); Sara Lipton, https://web.archive.org/web/20190204004728/https://www.nybooks.com/daily/2016/06/06/the-first-anti-jewish-caricature/ [accessed February 4, 2019].

of hours known as the Salvin Hours, dated to the 1270s, the convergence of the "hook-nosed" Jews and the figure of the demon becomes complete. The Jews represented alongside a placid and barefoot Jesus not only have grotesquely distorted noses, but also darker skins and grimacing mouths that betray the illuminator's desire to approximate them to demons rather than humans.[4]

Whilst the appearance of the caricatured "Jewish nose" in anti-Jewish iconography established an artistic trend that would gradually consolidate itself, it must be noted that its appearance was never as systematic in the medieval period as it later became in the nineteenth or twentieth centuries. The reason for this is not clear but it is possible to speculate that medieval segregationist legislation played a role in this. The need for caricatured noses was presumably lessened if Jews could be visually distinguished in paintings and illuminations by means of symbols (such as yellow circles) worn on their clothing or distinctive headgear like the "Jewish hat" that many were compelled to wear in parts of Europe, especially in the Holy Roman Empire (described as the *Judenhut* in German or *pileus cornutus* in Latin). The antisemitic fear in modern Europe of emancipated and assimilated Jews, who were no longer subject to such segregationist laws, may well have helped make the "Jewish nose" a constant feature of modern antisemitic iconography as modern propaganda seeking to insist that Jews were "different" sought inspiration in medieval art.

Perhaps the most bizarre aspect of the campaign to dehumanize the Jewish body beyond caricatured noses was the concept of Jewish "male menstruation" or that Jewish men suffered from periodic and bloody outbreaks of hemorrhoids. For the writer Caesarius of Heisterbach (ca. 1180-ca. 1240), Jews suffered from a "bloody flux" on Good Friday as a punishment for the crucifixion of Christ. Similarly, Thomas of Cantimpré (1201–1272) elaborated on this by asserting that the Jews had been cursed by a hereditary "bloody flux" in

---

4 British Library, Additional MS 48985, fol. 29r.

fulfilment of Matthew 27:25: ("His blood be upon us and upon our children") and only their acceptance of Christ would heal them in just the same way that Christ had healed the hemorrhaging woman (Luke 8:48). Further support for this belief was found in Psalms 77:66 and the punishment inflicted by God upon the enemies of his chosen people ("And he smote his enemies on the hinder parts: he put them to an everlasting reproach"). Beyond biblical explanations, other Christian writers attributed the Jews' chronic suffering of bloody hemorrhoids to their idleness and melancholic temperament as well as a divine curse. In 1221, the chronicler Jacques de Vitry (ca. 1165–1240) made the link between these explicit, noting that the Jews "have become unwarlike and weak even as women and it is said that they have a flux of blood every month. God has smitten them in their hinter parts, and put them to perpetual opprobrium."[5] In a Christian society and warlike culture that placed a premium on military prowess and valour, the idea of periodic bleeding by Jewish men akin to women's menstruation evidently feminized the Jew, rendering him even more ignoble and worthy of contempt.

The concept of the bleeding male Jew was likely linked with the notion that Jews, both male and female, possessed a repulsive smell, the supposedly distinctively "Jewish stench" (*foetor iudaicus*). Medieval authors assigned medical and theological significance to bodily odour. A foul bodily smell or odour was associated with diseases (such as leprosy) and contagion as well as being a symptom of bodily corruption due to sin (conversely the bodies of converts, martyrs, and saints emanated a sweet, pleasant odour). The xenophobic association of "otherness" and unpleasant odour is not unique to anti-Jewish folklore. The Dominican author Felix Fabri, writing in the 1480s, explained the ritual ablutions of Muslims by claiming that they exuded an "especially loathsome odour" whilst modern English folklore has associated

---

5 Irven M. Resnick. "Medieval Roots of the Myth of Jewish Male Menses," *The Harvard Theological Review*, 93, no. 3 (July 2000): 241–63.

Frenchmen with an unpleasant garlic smell due to their supposedly garlic-rich diet.[6]

In the case of medieval Jews, however, claims of a "Jewish stench" became extremely frequent from the thirteenth century to the extent that one modern historian has described it as "the first and most constant feature of anti-Judaism, and the most universal as well."[7] Medieval writers referred to the *foetor iudaicus* in a variety of contexts. Thus the Franciscan preacher Berthold of Regensburg (ca. 1220–1272) scolded his Christian listeners for their poor religious observance by noting that "now you see very well that a stinking goatish Jew, whose odor is offensive to all, honors his holy days better than you. Bah! As a Christian you should be ashamed of yourself that you do not trust in God as much as the stinking Jew." Similarly, Caesarius of Heisterbach, whom we have already mentioned above, featured the "Jewish stink" in an exemplary story about a Jewish girl who converted to Christianity and entered into a convent. When her family sought to remove her from the convent, Caesarius claimed, the daughter had noticed their "Jewish stench" before she had even seen them.[8]

It is striking that the two authors cited above were not writing theological treatises. Their works were instead addressed to novices in monasteries and common people. The theme of the "Jewish stink" (as well as "Jewish noses" and "Jewish male bleeding") was thus one that particularly came to the fore in a specific context: when churchmen were reaching out to a more "popular" audience, one that was considered "less learned" and for whom theologically focused polemics would have held little interest.

Finally, the "Jewish stink" may well have been linked in popular folklore with the association of Jews and two animals:

---

6 Irven M. Resnick, *Marks of Distinction: Christian Perceptions of Jews in the High Middle Ages* (Washington, DC: Catholic University of America Press, 2012), 239–40.

7 Claudine Fabre-Vassas, *The Singular Beast: Jews, Christians, and the Pig* (New York: Columbia University Press, 1999), 103.

8 Resnick, *Marks of Distinction*, 237–38.

the goat and the pig. The horned goat was easily associated with the Devil and, as early as 447, a church council held at Toledo (Spain) had described the Devil as a creature with animal attributes including horns, cloven feet, and a sulphurous smell. It is therefore not surprising that Jews are frequently portrayed in late medieval Europe riding on those animals, especially in Christian iconography. The *Judensau* (Jew's sow)—the portrayal of Jews riding on female pigs, suckling at their udders, and either eating their excrement or kissing the animals' anus—became a popular iconographical motif in the medieval German-speaking lands of the Holy Roman Empire (see Figure 2). From the early fourteenth century onwards, the *Judensau* appears in woodcut images produced for a popular audience as well as sculptures carved out of stone or wood, most notably outside the church of Wittenberg and on the choir stalls of Cologne Cathedral. It was nothing less than a deliberate attempt to ridicule Jews by associating them not only with an animal known to wallow in filth and which the Jews were known to shun for religious reasons, but also a crude polemical attack on the Talmud and rabbinical Judaism to which the sow and her milk/excrement are compared.[9]

The Host Desecration Libel

If the Jews were effectively dehumanized by the emergence of myths and caricatures about their bodies, their demonization was more dependent on their representation as existential threats to both the Church and ordinary Christian men, women and children. Just as witches and heretics were accused of making pacts with the Devil and seeking to harm Christian society, Jews would likewise come to be systematically accused in popular folklore and the writings of some churchmen from the twelfth century onwards of seeking to achieve the same ends.

---

9 Isaiah Shachar, *The Judensau: A Medieval Anti-Jewish Motif and Its History* (London: Warburg Institute, 1974).

Figure 2. The *Judensau*: Jews Suckling a Sow.
Woodcut from Kulturhaus Wittlich, the former Synagogue in
Wittlich, Rheinland-Pfalz, late fifteenth century. From Wikimedia
under GNU Free Documentation Licence.

Anxieties about the vulnerability of sacred objects falling into
the power of Jews can be found in the early medieval period.
The Gallo-Roman bishop Gregory of Tours (538/39–594)
wrote a work on the glory of Christian martyrs in which he
recorded a story of Jewish sacrilege. According to Gregory, a
Jew angered by the servile status of Jews, stole into a Church
at night and stabbed an image of Christ that miraculously
bled. He attempted to take the image home to destroy it but
the trail of blood allowed the Christians to track him down,
rescue the image and put the sacrilegious Jew to death.
This strange story, regardless of whether bishop Gregory
invented it himself or whether he was merely repeating oral
folklore, rapidly gained traction in the Christian world with
different variations appearing. In a homily entitled *De Passio
Imaginis Domini Nostri Jesu Christi* and attributed to St. Atha-
nasius of Alexandria (ca. 296/98–373) though doubtless from
a much later date, it was claimed that in the city of Beirut (in

modern-day Lebanon) some Jews had discovered an image of Christ which they had proceeded to mistreat and insult. When pierced with a lance, the statue had miraculously produced blood that could heal the sick, leading to the conversion of the Jewish iconoclasts.[10]

Whilst accusations of image desecration existed in the early modern period, they were never as common as in the central and later medieval period. From the twelfth century onwards, Jews were repeatedly accused not just of dese-crating crucifixes but also chalices and images of Christ or the Virgin Mary. The narrative nevertheless also acquired a new element. One of the most common accusations levelled against the Jews in this later period was that they actively sought to enact their hatred of Christians through acts of desecration inflicted upon the holiest object that could be found in churches: the consecrated host (bread). Belief in the miracle of transubstantiation—the Catholic doctrine that the bread and wine used in the communion become the actual flesh and blood of Jesus Christ after they are consecrated by the priest during mass—became the subject of controversy in the eleventh century and a doctrine of the Church in the thirteenth century. The link between these developments and the accusations made against Jews in the twelfth century seems clear: if the Jews sought to desecrate the consecrated bread then this was also further proof of the miracle of tran-substantiation, especially when the narrative includes the miraculous conversion of obdurate Jews.

Versions of the host desecration story appear in the writ-ings of churchmen throughout medieval Latin Europe: from England to Italy and from Spain to Poland (see Figure 3). The most notorious, though not the first, was the 1290 host des-ecration libel of Paris, which became the archetype for many more libels in the following centuries. The story has come

---

10 Miri Rubin, *Gentile Tales: The Narrative Assault on Late Medieval Jews* (New Haven: Yale University Press, 1999), 8–9; Katherine Aron-Beller, "ByzantineTales of Jewish Image Desecration: Tracing a Narrative," *Jewish Culture and History* 18, no. 2 (2017): 209–34.

down the centuries in many slightly different versions but the common narrative thread is that, just before Easter Sunday, a Jewish moneylender and pawnbroker named Jonathan allegedly induced one of his debtors, a Christian woman, to secretly steal a consecrated host and hand it over to him. In exchange for betraying her Lord Jesus Christ and handing him over his "enemies," like Judas, the Jew promised to return the clothes she had pawned. When this transaction was carried out, Jonathan locked himself in his family home and proceeded to desecrate the host by stabbing it. Since he was unable to cut it into pieces, he was seized by an uncontrollable fury, a madness that caused him to scourge the host and pierce it with a spear. The host miraculously bled and the Jew cast it into boiling water without being able to destroy it. Instead of disintegrating, the host rose from the water and turned into an image of Christ. The crime was discovered when the Jew's young son unintentionally revealed the goings-on in a conversation held in the street with another Christian woman, who alerted the Christian authorities. Alerted to the sacrilege, the authorities arrested the Jew, his wife and family and returned the host to the church of *Saint-Jean-en-Grève*. Whilst the wife and children converted to Christianity, the unrepentant Jonathan refused and was burned at the stake.[11]

The story of the 1290 host desecration libel was an exemplary one, designed to convince the faithful of the genuine presence of Christ in the consecrated communion wafer through a narrative that features stock characters repeated in all host desecration libels: the sinful Christian woman/man who betrays Christ, the "evil" Jewish male who desecrates the host and is justly punished for it, the pious and righteous Christian woman/man who rescues the host, and the miraculous conversion of the Jewish wife and children. At the core of the host desecration narrative, however, lies a collective demonization of the "Jewish other." The constant retelling of the host desecration libel in oral stories, written accounts, and visual artworks produced across Europe created an image of

11 Rubin, *Gentile Tales*, 40–44.

Figure 3. Host Desecration. Medieval painting of host desecration by Jews, from the Museu Nacional d'Art de Catalunya, Barcelona. Ca. 1335–1345 108.8 × 222 × 8.7 cm (panel within the whole). Inventory number: 009920-000. From the chapel of Corpus Christi in the church of the monastery of Santa Maria de Vallbona de les Monges (Urgell). Tempera, stucco reliefs, gold leaf and varnished metal plate on wood.

collectively fanaticized Jews whose systematic desecration of consecrated hosts was nothing less than an organized religious ritual. The 1290 host desecration libel involved a single Jew and his family but later allegations implicated groups of Jews and sometimes even entire Jewish communities. Moreover, the alleged desecration was no longer just performed in private homes but in synagogues, another element in the narrative that implied collective Jewish action and guilt. This was especially the case in the fifteenth century. In the Spanish town of Segovia an accusation in 1410 led to an outbreak of violence and the confiscation of the community's synagogue (which was turned into the Church of the Corpus Christi, the feast of the eucharist). Similarly, the 1477–78 host desecration libel of Passau in Germany, for example, broadly followed the traditional narrative but implicated a large number of Jews in the town. The synagogue of Passau was demolished and replaced with a church dedicated to Christ the Saviour. The emergence of the host desecration libel had very real and terrible consequences for many Jewish communities in Europe. Such accusations were often followed by judicial executions and in some cases by outbreaks of popular violence leading to the massacre of entire communities such as during the Rintfleisch massacres of 1298 in Germany or the Brussels massacre of 1370 in the Low Countries. In its most extreme form, the 1490–1491 story of the Holy Child of La Guardia in Spain, the host desecration libel coalesced with allegations of witchcraft and another potent element in the medieval anti-Jewish narrative: the Blood Libel.[12]

Ritual Murder: The Blood Libel

The medieval "Blood Libel"—the claim that Jews ritually abduct, torture, and murder Christian children in order to parody the crucifixion of Christ and/or harvest their blood with the aim of manufacturing unleavened bread for Passover supposedly in accordance with Talmudic injunctions or to con-

---

12 Rubin, *Gentile Tales*.

duct black magic—was the most extreme manifestation of popular anti-Jewish beliefs in the medieval period.

Historians still debate the origins of the Blood Libel and the reasons for its appeal. For some, it is linked to an increasing focus on the Passion of Christ in medieval theology and the cult of the Holy Innocents, others prefer to see it as part of the association, in Christian eyes, of Jews with magic in general and black magic in particular, whilst a number of sociologists have examined possible psychological explanations.[13] In practice, there was always a specific context underpinning the rise of the accusation in a specific European location such as an ambitious bishop seeking to establish a lucrative saintly cult or a conflict in jurisdiction between the crown and a town's inhabitants.

The first cases in the twelfth century involved claims that Jews had abducted young boys in order to gruesomely murder them in a macabre parody of the crucifixion of Christ. The most noted of these early cases include the murders of William of Norwich in England and Richard of Pontoise in France. The accusation developed an even more sinister and serious character in the thirteenth century. In 1235, outside of the town of Fulda in central Germany, the five sons of a miller were killed when their father's mill caught fire whilst their parents were in the town. The contemporary chronicles state that the townsfolk rapidly blamed the Jews of Fulda for the deaths and murdered thirty-four of them in revenge. What is special about the Fulda Blood Libel, however, is that for the first time the Jews were accused of having slaughtered the children to collect their blood before burning the mill to conceal their crime. When the tumult menaced to spread to other towns, the Holy Roman Emperor Friedrich II was compelled to intervene to protect the remaining Jewish communities in Germany that were under his personal protection.

The chronicle accounts of the Blood Libel at Fulda offer few details about the event itself beyond the facts listed above but the investigation called by Friedrich II is enlightening. It makes

---

13 See *The Blood Libel: A Casebook in Anti-Semitic Folklore*, ed. Alan Dundes (Madison: University of Wisconsin Press, 1991).

it clear that the allegation that Jews had murdered children to harvest their blood was linked to a belief that they were acting in accordance with a Talmudic injunction. The Emperor ordered Jewish converts to Christianity and "many experienced experts in Jewish law" to provide their opinion "whether there survives any belief leading to the perpetrating of any act regarding human blood, which might impel the Jews to commit the aforesaid crime." The authorities consulted (who are not named) rightly pointed to the absolute prohibition of the consumption of blood in Jewish dietary regulations. Consequently, in 1236, Friedrich pronounced the Jews "absolved of this imputed crime" and threatened punishments against Christians who accused Jews of the Blood Libel. Although Friedrich's decree does not reveal any more precise details of the events at Fulda, it is clear on one capital point: the accusations circulating in the German lands of the Holy Roman Empire in the 1230s now linked the Talmud to the ritual slaughter of Christian children. Moreover, the accusation spread across Europe and increased in frequency despite an official condemnation by the papacy of a case in southern France in 1247. It took some time for the linking of the Jewish faith and rituals on one hand and the accusations of ritual murder and cannibalism on the other hand to become a standard feature of the ritual murder libel. Most accusations of ritual murder in the century after Fulda—such as the alleged martyrdom in 1255 of the English child-"saint" Hugh of Lincoln—continued to revolve around the notion that Jews sought to ridicule/parody the Passion of Christ although claims that the Jews indulged in black magic also appeared. The chronicler Matthew Paris claimed that Jews had murdered and dismembered Hugh of Lincoln "for what reasons we do not know, but it was asserted to be for the purpose of practicing magical operations."[14]

By the fourteenth century, allegations of ritual murder began to feature claims that Jews needed the blood of Chris-

---

14 For an analysis of these cases of Blood Libel and English translations of the original documents see Darren O'Brien, *The Pinnacle of Hatred: The Blood Libel and the Jews* (Jerusalem: Magnes, 2011).

tian children to produce *matzah* (unleavened flatbread) for the Passover festival or to manufacture magical remedies. The claims became a core feature of the libel in the fifteenth century, especially in the lands of the Holy Roman Empire. During the Blood Libel cases of Endingen (1470), Trent (1475), Regenburg (1476), and Freiburg (1503), torture was used to extract confessions from Jews. The printing press assisted the spread of the accusation of the ritual murder of Simon of Trent in 1475 through cheap pamphlets and woodcuts featuring distressing representations of Simon's martyrdom. Simon of Trent became the most infamous and widely reported case, partly because of Trent's location on the linguistic German–Italian borderlands and on a major commercial artery and pilgrimage road connecting Germany and Italy. Moreover, anxious to establish a lucrative saintly cult, the ambitious local bishop fought off early papal attempts to reprimand him. In 1478 the bishop even obtained a papal bull confirming that the trials and executions of the Jews had been conducted in accordance with legal procedures although the papacy sought to dissuade any further anti-Jewish violence by noting the earlier papal decree of 1247. Eventually, however, the cult of Simon of Trent as a martyr of the Church was recognized by the papacy in 1588 (see Figure 4).[15]

The most extreme and bizarre medieval case of Blood Libel was without doubt that of the so-called Holy Child of La Guardia in central Spain. In 1490, a group of Jews and Jewish converts to Christianity were arrested and accused by the Spanish Inquisition of a horrifying plot. The conspiracy involved a plan to steal a consecrated host and mix it with the heart of a small child they had kidnapped, ritually tortured, and murdered beforehand with the objective of concocting a poison that would kill all the Christians in Spain. Although no missing child was reported, and no corpse of a child was

---

15 See the studies of Ronnie Po-Hsia, *The Myth of Ritual Murder: Jews and Magic in Reformation Germany* (New Haven: Yale University Press, 1988) and *Trent 1475: Stories of a Ritual Murder Trial* (New Haven: Yale University Press, 1992).

Figure 4. The Blood Libel: Martyrdom of Simon von Trent, depiction from the *Nuremberg World Chronicle* by Hartmann Schedel (1493). Available online at https://commons.wikimedia.org/wiki/Category:-Simon_of_Trent#/media/File:Ritualmord-Legende.jpg.

ever found, the Inquisition proceeded with a trial that ended with confessions extracted under torture, the burning of the arrested men, and the cult of a "child martyr" that still endures today in the village of La Guardia.[16]

The blood libel was the ultimate form of demonization to which Jews were subjected in the medieval period. The notion of a ritual form of cannibalism involving the torture and gruesome murder of young, innocent Christian children placed the figure of the Jews on a similar level to that of witches. Indeed the most celebrated treatise on witches printed at the end

---

16 Henry Charles Lea, "El Santo Niño de la Guardia," *The English Historical Review* 4, no. 14 (April 1889): 229–50.

of the medieval period, the 1487 *Malleus maleficarum* of the Dominican Heinrich Kramer, similarly accused witches who had made a pact with the Devil of infanticide and cannibalism. Moreover, the notion Jews needed Christian blood to celebrate the Passover festival meant that ritual murder and cannibalism were portrayed as an integral part of rabbinical Judaism.

The "Jewish Conspiracy" against Christendom

At the basis of the medieval host desecration accusations and the Blood Libel lies a notion that has become a mainstay of modern western antisemitism: Jews are intrinsically evil, they are a foreign body within Christian society, and they all secretly plot to destroy Christianity and their host Christian societies. Their horrifying crimes are not the crimes of individual Jews or even individual communities but rather ones for which all Jews are responsible. If many medieval Christians saw the world as one in which the forces of Satan constantly endeavoured to undermine the Christian faith and Christian society, it is hardly surprising than the Jews came to be assigned a role in this demonic conspiracy.

Since the early twentieth century, the forged *Protocols of the Elders of Zion* have given antisemites across the world the "evidence" that they need to establish the existence of a worldwide "Jewish conspiracy." The medieval period did not have any forgery akin to the *Protocols* but it is possible to discern the emergence of the idea of a wide-ranging secret Jewish conspiracy seeking bring about the collapse of the Christian West and even the existence of forged documents supporting such a claim.

This concept of a collective Jewish conspiracy against Christians is plainly stated in the work of Thomas of Monmouth, the twelfth-century English monk who wrote the hagiography of the first blood libel victim, William of Norwich. Claiming to be acting on information received from a converted Jew named Theobald, Thomas of Monmouth told his readers that "in the ancient writings of their ancestors it was written that Jews could not achieve their freedom or ever return to the lands of their fathers without the shedding of human blood." Accordingly, a yearly council of "the chief men and rabbis of the Jews who dwell in Spain" was held in the town of Narbonne where lots were cast to select one of the Jewish communities scattered across the world and "whichever region was chosen by the lot, the capital city had to apply that lot to the other cities and towns, and the one whose name comes up will carry out that business."[17] Likewise, the English chronicler Matthew Paris emphasized in the thirteenth century that "almost all the Jews of England agreed to the murder [of Hugh of Lincoln]" and that every year the Jewish communities all sent representatives to a secret gathering where the Christian child was gruesomely murdered.[18]

The trope of a Jewish conspiracy in the medieval period frequently involved the concept of a Jewish–Muslim alliance with the Jews playing the role of a fifth column within Christendom. In thirteenth-century Spain, the 1236 chronicler Lucas de Tuy (?–1249) claimed that the Jews had played a major role in the Muslim conquest of the Iberian Peninsula in 711 by betraying the important town of Toledo into their power.[19] Although the claim has no historical support, and had its critics, it became a recurring theme in medieval and modern Spanish historiography. The notion of a Jewish–Muslim alliance was appealing because of the perceived antagonism of both these groups to Christianity. Some medieval Christian theologians argued that Islam was itself a "Jewish invention," created by Jews (sometimes with the help of heretics) to destroy Christianity. As early as the twelfth century, Abbot Peter the Venerable of Cluny, who commissioned the first known Latin translation of the Quran, stated that Muhammed had been influence by Jews and heretics. Later in the fifteenth century, the German theologian Nicholas of Cusa (1401–1464)

---

17 Thomas of Monmouth, *The Life and Passion of William of Norwich*, ed. Miri Rubin (London: Penguin, 2014), 61–62.

18 O'Brien, *The Pinnacle of Hatred*, 314–16.

19 Lucy K. Pick, *Conflict and Coexistence: Archbishop Rodrigo and the Muslims and Jews of Medieval Spain* (Ann Arbor: University of Michigan Press, 2004), 175–76.

went even further by contending that the Jews had not only influenced Muhammed to create the Quran but that "three sly Jews" corrupted the text of the Koran after his death in order to make it particularly hostile to Christians.[20]

In France, however, it was not until the early fourteenth century that a conspiracist narrative involving Jews and other enemies of Christendom emerged during the 1320-1321 "shepherds' crusade," essentially a popular movement in France that began as a crusade to fight Muslims in Spain but ended as a rebellion against the French monarchy. As the "crusaders" marched south, they attacked two groups that shared the unhappy status of social outcasts: lepers and Jews. Jews were directly subject to royal authority and attacks on them were a way of challenging royal authority but the violence was justified by accusing them of having collaborated with Muslims to destroy Christianity by means of poison. In the case of the Jews, it was alleged that they had coordinated the plot and letters supposedly sent by the Jews to the Muslim rulers of Granada in Spain and "Babylon" (Cairo?) were produced. These letters, allegedly found in the house of a Jew, claimed that the Muslim rulers had agreed to convert to Judaism and restore Jerusalem once the Jews had successfully persuaded the lepers to poison the water supply of Christians.[21]

These forgeries are historically significant as they offer evidence of a conscious desire, similar to that underpinning the creation of the later *Protocols*, to convince Christians of the genuineness of the supposed conspiracy through documents presented as produced by Jews, purportedly secret and never intended to be read by Christians, and thus wor-

---

20 Peter the Venerable, *Against the Inveterate Obduracy of the Jews*, ed. Resnick, 23 and 33; Jasper Hopkins, *Nicholas of Cusa's De pace fidei and Cribratio Alkorani: Translation and Analysis* (Minneapolis: Banning, 1990), 79.

21 Malcolm Barber, "Lepers, Jews and Moslems: The Plot to Overthrow Christendom in 1321," *History* 66 (1981): 1–17 doi:10.1111/j.1468-229X.1981.tb01356.x.

thy of credit. In the fantasized Christian conspiracy theory of 1321–1322 another idea is articulated: that the Jews were more dangerous than any other group threatening Christianity. A higher rank in the hierarchy of Christianity's enemies is assigned to Jews rather than to Muslims or lepers. This is not surprising given that some Christian theologians had already expressed the belief that the persistent refusal of Jews to acknowledge Christianity's truth made them worse than other non-Christians. Already in the twelfth century, Peter the Venerable described the Jews as "vile blasphemers, worse than any Saracens," to which he also added a further specification: that they had become "worse than pagans and worse even than demons."[22]

The period after 1321 witnessed a gradual escalation of extreme conspiracy theories involving Jews. The outbreak of the great pandemic in the fourteenth century—the Black Death of 1346–1353—that caused the deaths of millions gave rise to further elaborations on the theme of a Jewish conspiracy. Outbreaks of anti-Jewish violence in France during the mysterious but deadly plague, that medieval medical knowledge was powerless to stop, were driven by claims that the Jews had caused the plague by poisoning wells used by Christians. The theme of a conspiracy involving Jews living across Christendom was one that reappeared in such a context. Following the arrest and interrogation of Jews in the castle of Chillon on suspicion of poisoning wells in Switzerland and Savoy, it was alleged (and confessions were accordingly obtained through torture or fear), that they had been acting under precise instructions from Spain. The head conspirator was supposed to have been a certain Rabbi Jacob of Toledo, who had also provided the local Jews, and other Jews in the region, with a special poison.[23] Two centuries later, the readers (and presumably also listeners) of an anonymous German

---

22 Peter the Venerable, *Against the Inveterate Obduracy of the Jews*, ed. Resnick, 23 and 33.

23 Justus C. F. Hecker, *Der Schwarze Tod im vierzehnten Jahrhundert* (Berlin: Herbig, 1832), 97–102.

rhyming pamphlet entitled *Entehrung Mariä durch die Juden* (1515) attributed to the Franciscan polemicist Thomas Murner (1475-1537), were informed that the Jews of the "Spanish lands" (*hyspanier landt*) had held a "synod" (*concilium*) in which they had decreed that all Jews must consume Christian blood in their unleavened bread during Easter.[24] Finally, writing in the 1450s or 1460s, Friar Alonso de Espina envisioned an embattled "Fortress of Faith," the Church and Christian society—besieged by a coalition of its enemies, with the Jews foremost among them.[25]

Conclusion

By 1500, a form of popular anti-Jewish Christian discourse had emerged in Western Europe that presented a classic case of victim–perpetrator inversion. Despite the fact that Jewish communities throughout Western Europe were increasingly subjected to popular violence, official persecution, segregationist legislation or even expelled, it was the Christian community that was presented as threatened and under attack. The Jews were not normal human beings but monstrous, bloodthirsty creatures, working secretly and tirelessly in league with their lord the Devil and his other minions. Despite their small numbers, these pitiless Jews threatened not only the Church but also the life of every single Christian man, woman, and child. These fantasies stripped Jews of any individual identity and the Jews became a malignant satanic collective residing within Christian society, consumed by a hatred of Christians that was enacted in iconoclastic sacrilege and (sometimes cannibalistic) ritual murder. Rabbinic Judaism, was in effect reduced to a caricatured death cult.

---

24 Adam Klassert, "Die Entehrung Mariä durch die Juden: eine antisemitische Dichtung Thomas Murners," *Jahrbuch für geschichte, sprache und literatur Elsass-Lothringens* 21 (1905): 78–155 at 135.

25 Alonso de Espina, *Fortalitium fidei contra judeos, sarracenos aliosq[ue] christiane fidei inimicos* (Nuremberg: Koberger, 1494).

Some of these medieval tropes eventually declined in significance, namely the host desecration libel and the myth of Jewish male menstruation. Others, however, have prospered endured and proved surprisingly adaptable: the iconography of the "Jewish nose," the portrayal of Jews as dirty, the Blood Libel, and the concept of a worldwide Jewish conspiracy and alliance with the other enemies of Christianity. These have become constituent parts of modern antisemitic discourse not just in the West but increasingly in the Islamic world as the Israeli-Palestinian conflict stirs up anti-Jewish propaganda that often seemingly seeks its inspiration in the West. Such tropes have, of course, developed and adapted according to local contexts. Ritual murder allegations in Central and Eastern Europe during the late nineteenth and early twentieth centuries still insisted that the consumption of Christian blood was an integral part of Rabbinic Judaism but also sought proof of this through modern forensic science. Likewise, the medieval Jewish–Muslim or Jewish–Muslim–Leper conspiracy theory was replaced by a Jewish–Bolshevik–Freemason version more suited to Catholic or nationalist agendas in the modern era.

Chapter 4

Purity of Blood: An Iberian Exception?

The Jewish communities of the Iberian Peninsula had an origin story that placed their arrival in the peninsula after the destruction of the first temple in Jerusalem by the Babylonian King Nebuchadnezzar II in 587 BCE. Actual archaeological evidence (mostly tombstones), however, only testifies to their presence in the Iberian Peninsula during the Roman Empire and it is more likely that Jewish communities gradually established themselves in the Roman province of *Hispania* as the exiled Jewish diaspora spread across the Mediterranean following the destruction of the Second Temple by the Romans in 70 CE. Although they were persecuted during the post-Roman period in which the Christian Visigothic kings ruled the peninsula, the Jewish communities flourished economically and culturally in the wake of the Muslim invasion in 711 and Islamic takeover of most of the Iberian Peninsula. When the Muslim Umayyad caliphate of Cordoba collapsed in 1031, the various Christian kingdoms of the north (Portugal, Castile-León, Navarre and the Crown of Aragón) slowly began to expand southwards and increasing numbers of Jews came under Christian rule.

Until the end of the fourteenth century, Jews, Christians, and Muslims living in the various Christian kingdoms of the Iberian Peninsula coexisted in their daily lives—what historians have described as *convivencia*—although interfaith tensions always existed. The Jews who came under Christian rule were granted the same status as Jewish communities elsewhere in Christian Europe and their inferior status (relative to the dominant Christians) was enshrined in laws that threatened fierce punishments for Jews (and Muslims) whose actions threatened the religious status quo. Nonetheless, the frontier conditions in the Iberian Peninsula continued to create favourable economic conditions for Jews as Christian rulers, short of resources and manpower in their newly conquered lands, were keen to protect their Jewish subjects and to offer them inducements to remain under their authority.[1]

In comparison with the Jewish communities of other areas of Europe, the size of the Jewish population in the Iberian Peninsula appears to have been large. Although the available evidence is scant, it is sufficient to allow historians to confidently guestimate that there were around a quarter million Jews in Castile alone in the fourteenth century, a number that may well have approached three hundred thousand if Portugal and the lands of the Crown of Aragón are included. As late as 1492, after the adverse demographic impact of the Black Death and a wave of massacres and mass conversions, the number of Jews in the various Christian kingdoms of Spain was still around one hundred and fifty thousand. Moreover, documentary evidence shows that there were Jewish communities or residents in most Iberian towns. The number of Iberian Jews dwarfed that of the Jews in England in 1290 (ca. two thousand) and significantly exceeded that in France (ca. one hundred thousand in 1306) and Italy (ca. fifty to one hundred thousand).[2] The history of late medieval Iberian Jewry cannot, however, be straightforwardly incorporated within the wider

---

1 Jonathan Ray, *The Sephardic Frontier: The Reconquista and the Jewish Community in Medieval Iberia* (Ithaca: Cornell University Press, 2006).

2 Numbers sourced from Robin R. Mundill, *England's Jewish Solution: Experiment and Expulsion, 1262–1290* (Cambridge: Cambridge University Press), 26–27; Anna Foa, *The Jews of Europe after the Black Death* (Berkeley: University of California Press, 2000), 8–9; Joseph Pérez, *History of a Tragedy: The Expulsion of the Jews from Spain* (Urbana: University of Illinois Press, 2007), 14.

history of medieval European Jews and the situation in the Iberian Peninsula deserves to be examined separately.

The mass conversion of Jews following a wave of riots in 1391 and the resulting antagonism towards the neophytes and their descendants (the *conversos*) led to important developments in anti-Jewish hatred, especially the development of statutes of "purity of blood" (*limpieza de sangre*) that sought to exclude *conversos* from various institutions on the basis of their genealogical descent from Jews. Benzion Netanyahu, the author of a major but contested work on the origins of the Spanish Inquisition, has argued that antagonism towards the *conversos* was primarily racial and he readily uses the terms "race," "racism," "racists," and "antisemitism" in his work. Indeed, for Netanyahu, fifteenth-century Spain is of critical importance in the history of anti-Jewish sentiment since it witnessed "the rise of a strong racial movement" against Jewish converts to Christianity. In fifteenth-century Spain, Netanyahu argued, antipathy to the converts "ceased to rest mainly on religion [...] and centred on their "ethnic origin" as a major reason for the persecution." This "emergence of a theory of race" made Spain unique in medieval Europe for Netanyahu.[3] Historians have perceived Netanyahu's position as one motivated by a tacit ideological agenda seeking to underscore the pointlessness of assimilation by European Jews in the face of a historically continuous racial hatred of Jews by Gentiles.[4] As such, it is tempting to dismiss his claims and usage of "antisemitism" as anachronistic. Yet is there any merit behind the claim that events in Spain led the way in Europe, or at least made it a precursor, to the emergence of an explicitly racialized form of anti-Jewish hatred? Is the Iberian Peninsula an exception in medieval European history?

---

3 Benzion Netanyahu, *The Origins of the Inquisition in Fifteenth-Century Spain* (New York: New York Review Books, 1995), 1052–54 and 1144–45.

4 Brett Levinson, "On Netanyahu's *The Origins of the Inquisition in Fifteenth-Century Spain*: Does the Inquisition Justify Zionism?," *Journal of Spanish Cultural Studies* 6, no. 3 (2005): 245–58.

1391: The Iberian Watershed

Until the end of the fourteenth century, the story of Iberian Jewry does not differ markedly from that of the rest of Europe. Events in 1391, however, suddenly and brutally set it on a very different course. The vitriolic sermons of a Franciscan preacher in southern Spain, combined with the political instability of a child-ruler in Castile, led to the outbreak of a wave of anti-Jewish riots that spread across Castile and into the neighbouring Crown of Aragón. Crowds sacked Jewish quarters and some Jews were murdered but these riots differed from those that took place elsewhere in medieval Europe in one crucial aspect: they resulted in mass forced conversions as Jewish men, women, and children were dragged to churches and baptized under threat of death. In the decades that followed, a vigorous and coercive missionary campaign conducted by the Dominican St. Vincent Ferrer led to many more conversions. The exact number of Jews forced to convert to Christianity will never be known but it was very substantial, it can be reckoned in the thousands, possibly even the tens of thousands.[5]

The events of 1391 were unprecedented in European history. Once administered, the sacrament of baptism could not be rescinded and the reluctant Jewish converts could not return to Judaism after the riots had ended and the Crown had reasserted its authority. Whilst there had certainly been conversions to Christianity by Jews, there had never so many and in such a relatively short space of time. The result was that the converts and their descendants did not immediately assimilate into the wider Christian population. Unsurprisingly given the circumstances of their conversion, many amongst the "Old Christian" population regarded them with suspicion and suspected them of being judaizers: secret Jews who con-

---

5 Philippe Wolff, "The 1391 Pogrom in Spain. Social Crisis or Not?," *Past and Present* 50 (1971): 4–18; B. Gampel, *Anti-Jewish Riots in the Crown of Aragon and the Royal Response, 1391–1392* (Cambridge: Cambridge University Press, 2016).

tinued to observe their faith in private whilst pretending to be Christians in public. The neophytes and their descendants were generically referred to as "new Christians" (*cristianos nuevos*) or "converts" (*conversos*) for centuries after the events of 1391.[6]

In medieval Spain, the implications of the mass conversions in the wake of the riots of 1391 were enormous. The appearance of a large community of *conversos* transformed a society in which there had previously existed a clear distinction between Jew/Judaism and Christian/Christianity (and also Muslim/Islam). The actual religious beliefs of the *conversos*—especially the survival of crypto-Judaism—remain the object of considerable academic debate. What is beyond doubt, however, is that the former Jews found that their social position underwent a remarkable transformation. Unlike the remaining Jews of the Spanish kingdoms, who continued to be subject to segregationist laws and wore distinctive clothing as well as symbols, the *conversos* were no longer "conspicuous." They were free to seek careers and social advancement in the secular and ecclesiastical worlds and many of them did just that. Some ascensions were nothing short of spectacular. The erudite Rabbi Solomon ha-Levi of Burgos, a convert in 1391, took the name of Pablo de Santa Maria and rose to become the bishop of Cartagena in 1403 and then the bishop of Burgos in 1415. Other *conversos* rose to prominence in the worlds of commerce or royal administration. The rise of the *conversos* perhaps inevitably sparked resentment among many "Old Christians" which, when added to suspicions about the sincerity of their conversions, directly led to the birth of an Iberian phenomenon: the obsession with *limpieza de sangre*.[7]

---

6 David Nirenberg, "Mass Conversion and Genealogical Mentalities: Jews and Christians in Fifteenth-Century Spain," *Past and Present* 174 (2002): 3–41 at 40.

7 See Netanyahu. *The Origins of the Inquisition*, 3–213 and Norman Roth, *Conversos, Inquisition, and the Expulsion of the Jews from Spain* (Madison: University of Wisconsin Press, 1995), 15–87.

The "unfamiliar religious landscape" created by the events of 1391, to quote the historian David Nirenberg, caused many Christian Iberians to redefine their communal identity. Whereas religion had previously been sufficient, they now turned to genealogy, linking communal identities with existing notions of "caste," "race," and "nation."[8] To understand the concept of *limpieza de sangre*—which can be translated literally as "cleanliness of blood" but is more often rendered as "purity of blood"—it is important to grasp its medical foundations. Hippocratic/Galenic medical theory, which was prevalent in medieval Europe, held that men and women possessed the same genitalia, with the ovaries and uterus/vagina of a woman thought to be an inverted penis and testicles. The consequence was that both women and men were believed to produce semen/seed. The "seed" of a man and woman was essentially refined blood and, in its coalescence, hereditary traits were passed on to the child at the moment of its conception, creating its "nature." The "nature" of an individual was believed to include not just inherited physical characteristics but also hereditary behavioural/mental traits as well. Later, in the early seventeenth century, the famous lexicographer Father Sebastián de Covarrubias explained that an individual's *naturaleza* was indeed "the product of their caste or of their homeland or nation."[9]

Toledo, 1449: The Rise of *Limpieza de Sangre*

An uprising in the town of Toledo against King Juan II of Castile in 1449 was just as much an uprising by the "Old Christian" elite of the town against their *converso* rivals. The rebels expelled the crown's representatives and murdered a number of *conversos* whom they accused of being responsible for the imposition of a new and very unpopular royal tax. Once they were in control of the city, the rebels, led by Pero

---

8 Nirenberg, "Mass Conversion and Genealogical Mentalities," 40.

9 Sebastián de Covarrubias, *Tesoro de la lengua castellana, o española* (Madrid: Sanchez, 1611), letter N, 561r.

Sarmiento, issued a decree (*sentencia–estatuto*) banning *conversos* from public office:

> We, the said Pero Sarmiento [...] and the magistrates, knights, squires and citizens of the city [of Toledo], must and do declare, must pronounce and do pronounce and constitute and ordain and command that all the said converts, descendants of the perverse lineage of the Jews, in whatever guise they may be, both by virtue of canon and civil law, which determines against them in the matter declared above [exclusion from public office], and by virtue of the privilege given to this city by the said lord king of blessed memory, Don Alfonso, king of Castile and León, progenitor of the king our lord, and by other lords and kings their progenitors, and by his highness [the present king], sworn and confirmed as follows:

> Since by reason of the heresies and other offences, insults, seditions and crimes committed and perpetrated by them up to this day ... they should be had and held, as the law has and holds them, as infamous, unable, incapable and unworthy to hold any office and public or private benefice in the said city of Toledo and in its land, territory and jurisdiction, through which they might have lordship over Christians who are old believers [*sic*] in the holy Catholic faith of Our Lord Jesus Christ, to do them harm and injury, and thus be infamous, unable and incapable to give testimony on oath as public scribes or as witnesses, and particularly in this city; and by this, our sentence and declaration, following the tenor and form of the said privilege, liberties, franchises and immunities of the said city, we deprive them, and declare them to be and order that they be deprived of whatever offices and benefices that they currently hold [...].

> According to ancient chronicles, when this town was besieged by our enemies the Muslims (*moros*) led by their leader Tarife, after the death of the King Don Rodrigo, they entered into a treaty with the Muslims and betrayed the city [of Toledo] and its Christian inhabitants, and they allowed the Muslims to enter it as a result of which 306 old Christians of this city were put to the sword and more than 106 were taken out of the Church of Santa Leocadia

and enslaved [by the Muslims], including many men and women, old and young.[10]

The importance of the Toledan *sentencia-estatuto* lies in the way that discrimination between Christians was justified on the sole basis of genealogical descent. Linked to the "perverse lineage of the Jews," the *conversos* are held to be collectively guilty of the supposed crimes of their forebears, most notably the accusation that it was the Jews who betrayed Toledo to the Muslim invaders over seven centuries before. Moreover, the rebels in Toledo present the alleged secret judaizing of the *conversos*—their "heresies and other offences, insults, seditions and crimes committed and perpetrated by them up to this day"—as a collective offence for which they are all responsible. The conspiracist theme—the secret Jewish plot against the church waged by the *conversos*—was echoed in the propaganda produced by the Toledan rebels. A public proclamation written at the same time lamented that the "baptized Jews" were allowed to "kill the Old Christians" and seize their possessions whilst *converso* priests "yesterday taught in synagogues and today sing in churches" and "under the appearance and name of Christians are accustomed to inflict much harm and injuries upon true Christians."[11]

The rebels clearly realized that they were taking a momentous step by fundamentally contradicting one of the tenets of the Christian faith: St. Paul's unambiguous assertion that Christianity transcended ethnic divisions (Galatians 3:28). To legitimate their move, they needed a solid argument and they appealed to historical precedent. The reference to a supposedly similar privilege granted to Toledo by "the said lord king of blessed memory, Don Alfonso, king of Castile and León" seems to be a somewhat vague reference to a provi-

---

10 Translated by John Edwards, *The Jews in Western Europe 1400–1600* (Manchester: Manchester University Press, 2013), 100–102.

11 Eloy Benito Ruano, "El memorial contra los conversos del bachiller Marcos García de Mora," *Sefarad* 17 (1957): 314–51.

sion in the municipal law code (*fuero*) granted to the town by King Alfonso VII in 1118. The *fuero* in question stipulated that no Jews or recent Jewish converts ("ni judíos ni recién convertidos") should be granted power over Christians but it did not extend to a total ban on all descendants of Jews.[12] Beyond this, a rebel named Marcos García de Mora penned a memorial, essentially an appeal for support in which he advocated the need to "finish the persecution of that generation [of Jews]" (i.e., the expulsion or murder of all Toledan *conversos*). He marshalled a long list of accusations against the Jews and *conversos* and a host of arguments in support of the *sentencia-estatuto*. He did not use the expression "Jewish race" (*raza de judío*) but frequently used the expression "generation of Jews" or "descendants of the lineage of the Jews" to indicate the *conversos*, clearly marking their Jewish ancestry as their defining characteristic. García de Mora included inaccurate claims based on passages from Deuteronomy to justify the exclusion of *conversos* from office until "a certain generation" and a reference to Paul's Epistle to Titus (Titus 1:6–8). The Apostle Paul had stated that "a bishop must be blameless, as the steward of God; not self-willed, not soon angry, not given to wine, no striker, not given to filthy lucre." García de Mora interpreted this as a ban on bishops of Jewish origin and so he argued that the *conversos* should also be banned from positions of power because they possessed all these negative qualities "by their nature" (*por naturaleza*).[13]

The Toledan revolt was soon suppressed by King Juan II and the *sentencia-estatuto* was condemned by Pope Nicholas V. Papal condemnation, however, did not put an end to the "*converso* problem" and the tensions it generated. Less than two years later, in March 1451, a shift in domestic politics in Castile and the need to cultivate support in Toledo led King Juan II to reverse his earlier condemnation of the rebels and restore their "good reputation." Later that year, in November,

12 Roth, *Conversos, Inquisition, and the Expulsion of the Jews from Spain*, 90–91.

13 Benito Ruano, "El memorial contra los conversos."

the papacy issued a number of papal bulls. In one bull the papacy lifted its interdict on Toledo, absolving the reconciled Toledans of any wrongdoing whilst simultaneously calling for the establishment of an Inquisition to root out judaizing *conversos* of any rank. In the second bull, the pope reiterated the official position of the church regarding the equality of all Christians regardless of their origin. This ambivalence, together with the crown's own shifting position, marked a moral victory for the opponents of the *conversos* and was doubtless taken by many to represent a vindication of their beliefs/prejudices about *conversos*.

The idea that baptized Christians could be discriminated against merely on the basis of their Jewish ancestry was, unsurprisingly, a very controversial one. Important critics rose up to denounce ethnic discrimination and defend Christian unity. They included members of the clergy like the theologian Juan de Torquemada (1388–1468, not to be confused with the later infamous inquisitor Tomás de Torquemada), the *converso* Bishop Alfonso of Cartagena (1381–1456) and the Jeronymite Friar Alonso de Oropesa (?–1469). Their arguments, however, failed to stem the rising tide of suspicion and fear as the tensions between "Old Christians" and *conversos* grew more acute in the second half of the fifteenth century. Economic difficulties adversely affecting Castile and the weak rule of Juan II and his successor Enrique IV caused political instability that allowed anti-converso resentment to grow unchecked. At its most intense, anti-converso feeling manifested itself in renewed outbreaks of communal strife and rioting targeting *conversos* in 1467 and 1473–4.[14]

The *sentencia–estatuto* is significant because it was unprecedented in Western Europe. Its authors, a group of disgruntled townsmen who were certainly not members of a powerful ecclesiastical hierarchy, sought to implement the establishment of a state of permanent discrimination against a group of Christians on the sole basis of their Jewish ancestry. Their

---

14 Angus Mackay, "Popular Movements and Pogroms in Fifteenth-Century Castile," *Past and Present* 55 (1972): 33–67 at 59–60.

actions might have had little importance except for the failure of the papacy to maintain its initial unambiguous condemnation of their municipal decree. Moreover, their hatred of the "perverse lineage of the Jews" resonated in many parts of Castilian society.

Spain after 1449: Religion and Ethnicity Essentialized

It was also in the middle of the fifteenth century that one of the most successful anti-Jewish authors in late-medieval/ early-modern European was active: Alonso de Espina, the author of the infamous *Fortalitium fidei contra iudeos, saracenos aliosque christiane fidei inimicos* ("Fortress of Faith against Jews, Saracens and All Other Enemies of the Christian Faith"). Espina's book, already alluded to in Chapter 2, was written between 1458 and 1464 with the explicit aim of warning Christians about the dangers presented by the different enemies of the faith: Jews, heretics, Muslims, and demons. For Espina, these enemies of Christianity were all part of the Devil's wider conspiracy to destroy the church since, Espina writes: "the enemy is the heretic; the enemy is the Jew, the enemy is the Muslim; the enemy is the Devil." The *Fortalitium* offers its readers a compendium of anti-Jewish accusations of ritual murder, host desecration and various "cruelties" inflicted by Jews against Christianity and Christians. Beyond the Jews themselves, Espina also tackles judaizing *conversos* in the section of his work devoted to heretics, labelling them as the "worse heretics" (*peiores heretici*) and "more dangerous than the Arians and any others who have erred against the Christian faith." [15]

Espina's work offers an interesting case study of how important it is to analyse the rise of a proto-racialized anti-Jew-

---

[15] Rosa Vidal Doval. *Misera Hispania: Jews and Conversos in Alonso de Espina's Fortalitium Fidei* (Oxford: Society for the Study of Medieval Languages and Literature, 2013); Alonso de Espina, *Fortalitium fidei contra judeos* (1494), fols. 2r and 54v–55r.

ish sentiment in Spain in a nuanced manner. Understandably, many works of reference and scholars have been quick to present Espina as a rabid antisemite whose hatred of Jews was racial in character. The *Jewish Encyclopedia* (1906) described Espina as devoted to "the utter destruction of the Jewish race, Jews as well as Jewish converts to Christianity" and the historian Benzion Netanyahu asserted that Espina was "full of race hatred and race bias." A detailed examination of his work, however, reveals that his attitude towards the *conversos* was not so straightforward. Espina does not present the errors and crimes of the Jews and judaizing *conversos* as a consequence of genealogical determinism but rather as the result of their subjection to the Devil. Jews and judaizing *conversos* are not demonic because Judaism is a biological imperative but rather because they obdurately continue to believe in the "Law of Moses" and the Talmud and educate their children to become "Talmudists." Espina largely follows Nicholas of Lyra in expounding that genuine conversions can happen even though "great virtue in the heart is necessary" in the case of Jews, "who have been fed that [Jewish/Talmudic] doctrine since childhood."[16]

The reign of the *Reyes Católicos* Isabella of Castile and Ferdinand of Aragón restored political stability to the Spanish kingdoms from 1474 onward but did not lead to an abating of anti-*converso* prejudice. The striking similarity in which anti-*converso* and anti-Jewish sentiment was articulated in Spain can be demonstrated by citing the *Memorias* of the chronicler Andres Bernáldez (ca. 1450–1513). A curate in the south of Spain and chaplain of the archbishop of Seville, Bernáldez does not hold back in his verbal attack on *conversos*:

> [The *conversos*] did not believe in giving reward to God by means of virginity and chastity: all their effort was to grow and multiply. And during the time of the rise of this heretical depravity by *converso* gentlemen and merchants [in Seville], many monasteries were violated and many pro-

---

16 Soyer, "All one in Christ Jesus?"

fessed nuns corrupted and subjected to ridicule, some by bribes and some by deceptions, [these converts] not believing in or fearing excommunication. Rather, they did it all to injure Jesus Christ and the Church. And in general, for the most part, they were a profiteering people, with many arts and deceits, because they all lived from idle jobs and they had no conscience when buying or selling with Christians. They never wanted to take jobs such as ploughing or digging, or walking through the fields looking after flocks, nor did they teach such things to their children, but rather [they took] jobs in the town, and sitting down making their living with little effort. In these kingdoms, many of them gained great wealth and property in a short time, because they had no conscience about profit and usury, saying that they gained everything from their enemies, clinging to the saying that God ordered the people of Israel, in their departure to Israel, to rob Egypt by art and deceit, demanding from them as loans their vases and gold and silver cups.[17]

Conversos were thus tarred with exactly the same stereotypes—economic parasitism, licentiousness, usury, and hatred of Christianity—that had been the stock of anti-Jewish propaganda for centuries in Europe.

Perhaps the most evocative evidence in favour of continuity in Spanish anti-Jewish/anti-*converso* sentiment with the rest of Europe is survival of the host desecration and ritual murder libels, most notably the infamous case of the Holy Child of La Guardia. The story of the Holy Child of La Guardia combines the two mainstays of medieval anti-Jewish propaganda: the host desecration and ritual murder allegations. A *converso* returning from a pilgrimage to the shrine of Santiago was arrested in the town of Oviedo in 1490 after the discovery of a consecrated host in his luggage. Tortured by the Inquisition, the man "revealed" a devilish plot involving both Jews and judaizing *conversos*. The conspirators had allegedly kidnapped a four-year-old boy from his mother, ritually tortured him in a parody of the trial and passion of Christ before

---

17 Translated by Edwards. *The Jews in Western Europe 1400–1600*, 75.

killing him and extracting his heart, which they hoped to mix with the consecrated host in a potion that would kill all the Old Christians of the kingdom. The Inquisition, under inquisitor General Tomás de Torquemada, took control of the case and arrested the *converso* and Jewish suspects. Despite its inability to find any concrete evidence of a murdered or missing child—or any bereft parents—the Inquisition extracted confessions under torture that led to the burning of the prisoners in November 1491. The case of the Holy Child of La Guardia saw both Jews and *conversos* become the victims of irrational antisemitic fears. It is tempting to speculate that the newly established Inquisition exploited the whole incident to bolster its political position.[18]

On March 31, 1492, only four months after the surrender of the last Muslim stronghold of the Iberian Peninsula in Granada, Isabella and Ferdinand decreed that the Jews of their kingdoms must convert to Christianity or leave. Their edict is explicit about the motives behind this important decision: the Jews were expelled because their presence was held to be the main impediment to the religious assimilation of the Spanish *conversos*. Whilst there were still Jews around, the *conversos* could continue to judaize because they would have a direct access to Jewish teachings and knowledge about key aspects of the Jewish faith. "Informed by the inquisitors and by other devout persons, ecclesiastical and secular," the Spanish rulers lamented the failure of the segregationist laws and blamed the Jews for having "perverted and enticed" *conversos*, "to the great injury, detriment, and opprobrium of our holy Catholic faith."[19]

The expulsion of 1492 is yet another example of how complex anti-Jewish sentiment in fifteenth-century Spain was and how difficult it can be to categorize from a twenty-first century perspective. Was the expulsion edict an "antisemitic" act? Were Isabella and Ferdinand therefore "antisemites"?

---

18 Lea, "El Santo Niño de la Guardia."

19 Haim Beinart, *The Expulsion of the Jews from Spain* (Oxford: Littman Library of Jewish Civilization, 2002), 33–54.

On the one hand, they were ending the public toleration of Judaism and Jews but it is impossible to present the expulsion as an act motivated by a racialized hatred of Jews as an ethnic group deemed to be unassimilable. Jews were allowed to remain in Spain if they converted to Christianity. Moreover, on November 10, 1492 and July 30, 1493, the Spanish rulers offered a general safe-conduct to any Jews who had left their kingdoms and wished to return after converting to Christianity if they also brought back a certificate of their baptism. Upon their return to Spain, the converts would have the legal right to purchase back their property at the value at which it had been sold in 1492 (minus the value of any improvements made by the current owners). The new converts would be under royal protection and the safe-conduct promised that officials would assist them to collect debts that had been still outstanding at the time of their departure (minus any usurious interest). Any officials who did not assist the returnees or acted against them would incur a heavy fine.[20]

The antipathy of Isabella and Ferdinand to the Jews was not, it would thus appear, based on beliefs about genealogical determinism and "Jewish blood" but rather largely founded on a theological antagonism and their desire to ensure the complete assimilation of the *conversos* into the wider Christian population. The earlier establishment of the Spanish Inquisition in 1480 was, similarly, caused by a desire to root out any *conversos* who remained secretly faithful to Judaism ("judaizers") and enable the assimilation of those *conversos* who were genuinely Christian into the wider Christian population.

The relationship between Isabella and Ferdinand and the statutes of purity of blood is also a complex one. The regulations for the Inquisition that were printed in 1484 specified that the sons and grandsons of individuals convicted of heresy by the Inquisition, were prohibited from holding public office or becoming ordained priests as well as doctors, surgeons, apothecaries, and professional "bleeders" (*sangradores*). In the context of the 1480s this measure would obviously be

---

20 Beinart, *The Expulsion of the Jews from Spain*, 329–412.

targeting *conversos* but it kept the general term of heresy and was not an outright ban on all *conversos*. On September 10, 1501, Queen Isabella issued an edict banning all those convicted by the Inquisition of "heresy and apostasy," as well as the sons and grandsons "of those burned [for heresy]," from occupying positions of authority in royal and municipal government and extended the measure to any individuals seeking to work as physicians, surgeons, and apothecaries.[21] It would be easy to jump to conclusions and perceive this as evidence of their adoption of racialist views but this would be wrong. In fact, the inquisitors and the rulers of Castile and Aragón were merely adopting a well-established measure of Canon Law in which legal infamy was extended to the children and grandchildren of heretics. Moreover, it is important to note that neither of these measures amounted to an outright ethnic ban against all *conversos* since it only affected those convicted of judaizing as well as the following two generations of direct descendants.

Nevertheless, it must be recognized Isabella and Ferdinand did little to prevent the spread of *limpieza de sangre* statutes discriminating against *conversos* in some institutions. Statutes of *limpieza* were adopted by colleges in many Spanish universities, including the colleges of San Bartolomé at the University of Salamanca (1482); Santa Cruz at the University of Valladolid (1488), and San Antonio de Porta Coeli in the University of Sigüenza (1497).[22] Even the Spanish Inquisition, the institution tasked with ensuring the rooting out of judaizing *conversos*, embraced a racialized conception of judaizing. In 1494 the *Repertorium Inquisitorium*—a manual produced for

---

21 Miguel Eugenio Muñoz. *Recopilación de las leyes, pragmáticas reales, decretos, y acuerdos del Real Protomedicato* (Valencia: Bordazar, 1751), 71–74.

22 Baltasar Cuart Moner, *Colegiales mayores y limpieza de sangre durante la Edad Moderna. El estatuto de san Clemente de Bolonia (ss. XV–XIX)* (Salamanca: Universidad de Salamanca, 1991); Albert Sicroff, *Los estatutos de limpieza de sangre. Controversias entre los siglos XVI y XVII* (Newark, DE: Juan de la Cuesta, 2010), 123–30.

inquisitors and printed in the town of Valencia—specified that "the Jews transmit the perfidy of the Old Law [of Moses] to each other from father to son, through the blood."[23]

Whilst Isabella of Castile and Ferdinand of Aragón were the founders of the modern Spanish monarchy, there were two other independent kingdoms in the Iberian Peninsula: Navarre and Portugal. Aware that their assimilationist policies would fail if public Jewish worship was tolerated in both of these Iberian kingdoms, the *Reyes Católicos* subjected them to diplomatic pressure to follow the same policy. Portugal decreed the expulsion of its Jewish population in 1497 and Navarre the following year. In the case of Portugal, however, the Jewish population was never actually expelled but forced to convert to Christianity *en masse*. The result was the creation of a *"converso* problem" in Portugal very similar to that in neighbouring Spain as anti-*converso* resentment rapidly acquired proto-racial characteristics in the Lusitanian kingdom. Only two years after the forced conversion, the king of Portugal was already forced to grant a certificate to a convert and his family officially cleansing them of the "stain caused by their [Jewish] birth" and forbidding anyone from disdainfully calling them "New Christians." Within a decade, at Easter 1506, the streets of Lisbon would run with the blood of thousands of converts slain by rioting "Old Christians."

Conclusion

Was the Iberian Peninsula an exception? Was it an area where anti-Jewish sentiment morphed into a racialized antisemitism centuries before it did elsewhere in Europe because of an event that was unique to the peninsula: the mass conversion of Jews between 1391 and 1420 and the creation of a large population of converts that did not assimilate into the wider Christian population? The answer is not so clear-cut.

---

23 Louis Sala-Molins, *Le dictionnaire des inquisiteurs (Valence 1494)* (Paris: Galilée, 1981), 78.

The collective experience of Jews in the medieval Iberian Peninsula was undoubtedly different from that of their co-religionists elsewhere in Europe. The "*converso* phenomenon" rapidly caused anti-Jewish prejudices and hatreds in Spain to assume a proto-racialized character when these were transferred on to the neophytes and their descendants. Moreover, in comparison with the situation elsewhere in Europe, there can be no doubt that the emergence of a concept of *limpieza de sangre* clearly identifying belief in Judaism with "Jewish blood" sets medieval Iberia apart.

By the end of the fifteenth century and start of the sixteenth, however, the form of racialism that was targeting *conversos* was still developing. It did not fully mature until the early modern era and especially after 1550, with the spread of discriminatory statutes of *limpieza de sangre* to prestigious university colleges as well as orders of knighthood and cathedral chapters. The cathedral chapter of Toledo adopted statutes of purity of blood in 1547 that were approved not only by the Spanish Crown but by Pope Paul IV in 1555.[24] Anti-*converso* racialism would only find its fullest expression in the works of early modern polemicists who lobbied loudly for stricter statutes of *limpieza* or in some cases even the wholesale expulsion of the *conversos* from the Iberian monarchies. Prior to 1500, even an outspoken opponent of Jews and *conversos* like Fray Alonso de Espina did not openly embrace genealogical or biological determinism but blamed the obduracy of the Jews and judaizing of the *conversos* on the teachings of the Talmud.

Whilst the word *raza* existed in vernacular Spanish as early as the fourteenth century, its usage was largely confined to animal husbandry before 1500 or to denote hereditary traits (positive or negative). The negative usage of the expression *raza de judío*—"Jewish race"—only appears in the early modern period alongside other expressions linked to genealogical

---

24 Henry Kamen, *The Spanish Inquisition. A Historical Revision* (New Haven: Yale University Press), 236–9.

descent such as *casta de judío* ("Jewish caste"). The failure of the 1492 expulsion edict to bring an end to the "*converso* problem" allowed the development of a fully racialized antipathy towards *conversos*. Sebastian de Covarrubias' 1611 lexicon, for instance, defined a *Cristiano viejo* (Old Christian): as a "pure man" who does not possess any genealogical trace (*raza*) of Muslim or Jew. A *Cristiano nuevo* (New Christian or *converso*) was merely defined as "the contrary" of the above. Later in that century, the influential bishop Diego de Castejon y Fonseca (1580–1655) would argue that Judaism was a "venom" passed on hereditarily and the infamous polemicist Franciscan Fray Torrejoncillo would go so far as to warn his readers that any individual related to Jews within twenty-one degrees of consanguinity, was susceptible to develop negative Jewish character traits.[25] The emergence of the *limpieza de sangre* would also have repercussions beyond the Iberian Peninsula. Founded by St. Ignatius de Loyola in 1540, the Jesuit Order controversially adopted a decree (*De genere*) discriminating against the descendants of Jews (and Muslims) in 1593. The discriminatory decree remained in force (albeit moderated) until 1946 and in the modern era German and Italian antisemites seized upon it as a historical justification in their own propaganda.[26]

---

[25] Francois Soyer, *Popularizing Anti-Semitism in Early Modern Spain and its Empire: Francisco de Torrejoncillo and the Centinela contra Judíos* (1674) (Leiden: Brill, 2014), 19–46.

[26] Steiman, *Paths to Genocide*, 61–62; Kertzer, *The Popes against the*, 207 and 283–84.

Conclusion

It was noted in the first chapter of this book that many modern historians have described the use of the term "antisemitism" before the nineteenth century as an anachronism. These historians have argued that the history of anti-Jewish rhetoric should instead be divided into a "religious" pre-modern period and a "racial" modern period. In many respects, however, this is even more of a historical anachronism. Moreover, it is a dangerous anachronism since it has been conveniently used by modern Catholic and Protestant theologians and apologists to diminish or even negate the responsibility of their churches in the horrors of the twentieth-century holocaust.

The developments in anti-Jewish thought and rhetoric in the medieval period were, from the twelfth and thirteenth centuries onward, complex and cannot be labelled as merely amounting to an "anti-Judaism" based on a hostility to Judaism as a rival religious movement. Likewise, the concentration on race as the defining feature of modern antisemitism oversimplifies its multifaceted nature. Modern antisemitism has been, and continues to be, characterized by a range of beliefs that go beyond the obsession with defining Jews as a distinct race. These are (i) the fixation on a secret Jewish conspiracy to take political and economic control of the world by subverting Christian society; (ii) the belief that modern Jews follow a form of Judaism that has been perverted by the Talmud and which incites them to undermine Christian society and attack Gentiles in general and Christians in particular; and (iii) the equation of Judaism and Jewish ethnicity.

Whilst the medieval papacy was more-or-less consistent in espousing the Augustinian position of a grudging toleration of the Jews as a "witness people," it is important to note that its position was not always followed by many Christians, including many men of the Church. By the end of the medieval period, circa 1500, the notion that the Jews were intrinsically inclined to evil and the conflation of Judaism and Jewish ethnicity had become common across Europe. In a short pamphlet detailing a host desecration allegation printed in 1510, the German printer Hieronymus Höltzel, for example, asserted that a Jew attacking a consecrated host was acting out a "hate" and "envy" that was "congenital" (*angeboren*) among Jews.[1] Likewise, the statutes of *limpieza de sangre* that began to appear in the Iberian Peninsula in the fifteenth century offered an understanding of Judaism as a hereditary, biological character trait of the Jews, who transmitted it to their descendants through their "blood."

A number of early modern Christian polemicists, both Catholic and Protestant (including Martin Luther), adopted much of the existing medieval rhetoric demonizing the Jews and the Talmud, ensuring its transmission to the nineteenth century. The legacy of medieval ideas, concepts, and iconography is easy to discern in modern antisemitic propaganda. This can be found, for instance, in the enthusiastic endorsement of the Blood Libel in the Vatican newspaper *L'Osservatore Romano* in 1892, the writings of key antisemitic authors like the Frenchman Édouard Drumont, and, eventually, even in Nazi propaganda destined for mass popular consumption such as the children's picture books *Trau keinem Fuchs auf grüner Heid und keinem Jud auf seinem Eid* (Trust No Fox on his Green Heath and No Jew on his Oath, 1936), *Der Giftpilz* (The Toadstool, 1938) and the movie *Der ewige Jude* (The

---

I Hieronymus Höltzel, *Ein wunderbarlich Geschichte. Wye dye Merckischen Juden das hochwirdige Sacrament gekaufft, vnd zu martern sich vnderstanden* (Nuremberg: Höltzel, 1510).

Eternal Jew, 1940). During the Nuremberg Trials, *Der Giftpilz's* publisher and one of Nazi Germany's chief antisemitic propagandists, Julius Streicher, would argue that his prosecution amounted to a prosecution of Martin Luther, whose work he cited. In fact, Streicher was unwittingly acknowledging his debt to medieval Christian anti-Jewish thought and rhetoric, upon which Luther based his own writings. Even today, it is possible to find echoes of medieval prejudices and libels in such diverse media as white supremacist websites, ultra-traditionalist Catholic blogs, and extreme manifestations of anti-Israeli propaganda.

To argue that "antisemitism" began in 1879 when Wilhelm Marr first used the term or with the racial theories of the nineteenth century overlooks the fact that the origins of many of the key modern antisemitic tropes can be traced back to medieval ideas about Jews. Just as modern historians of "race" are increasingly noting that ethnic prejudice preceded modern theories of race by centuries, it is similarly important to note that the existence of a proto-racialized prejudice against Jews pre-dated the nineteenth century. If historians are increasingly willing to talk about the existence of "racisms" (plural), is it perhaps not also possible to discuss the existence of different "antisemitisms" (plural)?

To conclude, using the terms "antisemitic," "antisemite," or "antisemitism" in a medieval context may be jarring to some modern historians but their use offers a tool which historians can use to describe the formation of key concepts. Used wisely and contextually, "medieval antisemitism" (as opposed to just "antisemitism") can be a useful concept with which historians can designate a form of anti-Jewish hatred that was not simply religious in character and that prefigured "modern antisemitism" even though it did not possess the pseudo-scientific racial vocabulary and emphasis on the nation state of "modern antisemitism." It conveys the complexity of medieval Christian perceptions of Jews far more accurately than a simplistic dichotomy between a "religious Middle Ages" and a "racial modern period." Adding the qualifier "Christian" to "antisemitism" will also help to position the use of the term within a historical and religious framework in which extreme, proto-racialized forms of anti-Jewish hatred developed and became major influences on modern antisemitism. It is therefore the opinion of the author of this book that "medieval antisemitism" or perhaps "Christian antisemitism" are concepts that can be legitimately employed by historians in reference to some developments in the Middle Ages. This may not be a perfect solution but, as the name of the series in which this book is published suggests, history is imperfect.

Further Reading

The following moderately annotated list mentions titles in English that are particularly relevant to anyone interested in the subject of this book and that are generally widely available. The list is not meant to be comprehensive but to offer a list of works that will offer you an introduction to the topic.

Bethencourt, Francisco. *Racisms: From the Crusades to the Twentieth Century*. Princeton: University of Princeton Press, 2014.

> A ground-breaking work that challenges simplistic understandings of the concepts of "race" and "racism," arguing that there is no single, continuous tradition of racism in western history. Rather, ethnic prejudice preceded modern theories of race by centuries. A very useful book to help contextualize anti-Jewish sentiment in medieval Europe.

Chazan, Robert. *From Anti-Judaism to Anti-Semitism. Ancient and Medieval Christian Constructions of Jewish History*. Cambridge: Cambridge University Press, 2016.

> In this work, Chazan traced the evolving attitudes of Christian thinkers towards Jews and Judaism by focusing on a select number of texts from Antiquity to the dawn of the Reformation.

——. *The Jews of Medieval Western Christendom, 1000–1500*. Cambridge: Cambridge University Press, 2006.

> A concise survey of, and introduction to, the history of the Jewish communities established in western Christendom during the later medieval period.

—— . *Medieval Stereotypes and Modern Antisemitism*. Berkeley: University of California Press, 1997.

A very readable analysis of the different aspects of the hostile perception of Jews in medieval Europe.

Cohen, Jeremy. *The Friars and the Jews. The Evolution of Medieval Anti-Judaism*. Ithaca: Cornell University Press, 1982.

An impressive and comprehensive examination and analysis of the role played by the Franciscan and Dominican orders in the changing manner that Jews were perceived by Christian theologians and polemicists from the thirteenth century onwards.

—— . *Living Letters of the Law: Ideas of the Jew in Medieval Christianity*. Berkeley: University of California Press, 1999.

A detailed survey of the way that Christian thinkers from St. Augustine to St. Thomas Aquinas have perceived Jews and Judaism and the changes that occurred in the medieval period prior to 1300.

Dundes, Alan, ed. *The Blood Libel. A Casebook in Anti-Semitic Folklore*. Madison: University of Wisconsin Press, 1991.

A useful compilation of works by various authors on the subject of the Blood Libel from the medieval to the modern period.

Edwards, John, ed. and trans. *The Jews in Western Europe 1400–1600*. Manchester: Manchester University Press, 2013.

A broad-ranging collection of documents providing a vivid picture of the Jewish presence in European life during this period.

Fredricksen, Paula. *Augustine and the Jews. A Christian Defense of Jews and Judaism*. New Haven: Yale University Press, 2008.

A masterful analysis of Augustine's theological attitude towards Jews and Judaism that places Augustine's formulation of the status of Jews as a "witness people" within the context of his polemical writings against the heresy of Manichaeism.

Heng, Geraldine. *The Invention of Race in the European Middle Ages*. Cambridge: Cambridge University Press, 2018.

> This recent work forcefully challenges the notion that race did not exist prior to the nineteenth century and argues in favour of origins that can be traced back to medieval attitudes. Its second chapter examines attitudes towards Jews in medieval England as one of its case studies.

Hsia Po-Chia, R. *The Myth of Ritual Murder: Jews and Magic in Reformation Germany*. New Haven: Yale University Press, 1988.

> This pioneering work examines the rise and decline of Blood Libel accusations in Germany between ca. 1460 and the mid-sixteenth century.

Hsia Po-Chia, R. *Trent 1475: Stories of a Ritual Murder Trial*. New Haven: Yale University Press, 1992.

> A short but insightful analysis of the most infamous Blood Libel trial held in late medieval Europe.

Kertzer, David. *The Popes against the Jews: The Vatican's Role in the Rise of Modern Anti-Semitism*. New York: Knopf, 2001.

> Even though this book does not examine the medieval period, it offers a useful analysis of the modern papacy's attitude towards Jews that will be helpful to medievalists seeking to understand the long-term repercussions of the relationship between Jews and the papacy in the Middle Ages.

Langmuir, Gavin. *Toward a Definition of Antisemitism*. Berkeley: University of California Press, 1990.

> A crucial book for those interested in the subject of this book, in which Langmuir sets out his contentious argument in favour of "medieval antisemitism" by elaborating on the distinction between Anti-Judaism and antisemitism.

Lipton, Sara. *Dark Mirror: The Medieval Origins of Anti-Jewish Iconography*. New York: Metropolitan, 2014.

> A nuanced examination of the representation of Jews in Christian iconography during the central Middle Ages (1000–1300). This work argues that, in its initial stages, the stereotyping of

such representations was not linked to anti-Jewish sentiment but rather to the need to inspire Christian devotion.

Marcus, Kenneth L. *The Definition of Anti-Semitism*. Oxford: Oxford University Press: 2015.

Although this work focuses on modern developments—particularly on the controversial linking of antisemitism and Anti-Zionism after the creation of the state of Israel—it provides a very useful overview of some of the theoretical problems that historians face when seeking to define antisemitism.

Netanyahu, Benzion. *The Origins of the Inquisition in Fifteenth-Century Spain*. New York: New York Review Books, 1995.

A monumental (1384 -page) and exhaustive study of the origins of anti-*converso* sentiment in medieval Spain and, by extension, the origins of the Spanish Inquisition. Controversial amongst historians as its author argues that the *conversos* were genuine Christians persecuted for racial rather than religious reasons.

Nirenberg, David. *Anti-Judaism: The Western Tradition*. New York: Norton, 2013.

An exhaustive examination of the manner in which Jews and Judaism, and hostility to them, have become a constituent element of Western culture from Antiquity to the present.

Novikoff, Alex. *The Medieval Culture of Disputation. Pedagogy, Practice, and Performance*. Philadelphia: University of Pennsylvania Press, 2013.

A well-researched exploration of the culture of religious disputation in the High Middle Ages that became a central part of the attacks against Jews and Judaism in Paris (1240) and Barcelona (1263).

Ray, Jonathan. *The Sephardic Frontier: The Reconquista and the Jewish Community in Medieval Iberia*. Ithaca: Cornell University Press, 2006.

A balanced analysis of the status of Iberian Jews in the "frontier world" of medieval Iberia between 1000 and 1300.

Rose, E. M. *The Murder of William of Norwich: The Origins of the Blood Libel in Medieval Europe*. Oxford: Oxford University Press, 2015.

A remarkably detailed analysis of the first ritual murder allegation and reconstruction of the social and religious context in within it occurred.

Roth, Norman. *Conversos, Inquisition, and the Expulsion of the Jews from Spain*. Madison: University of Wisconsin Press, 2002.

A detailed analysis of the history of the Spanish *conversos* from 1391 until 1492. Argues that the *conversos* were not secret Jews but rather sincere Christians.

Rubin, Miri. *Gentile Tales: The Narrative Assault on Late Medieval Jews*. New Haven: Yale University Press, 1999.

A thought-provoking analysis of the host desecration libel that covers most of medieval Europe and seeks to explain how the narrative of host desecration became such a popular one.

Steiman, Lionel B. *Paths to Genocide. Antisemitism in Western History*. New York: St. Martin's, 1998.

A concise survey of "Jew-hatred" in the West from the early church to the Holocaust. This book will be useful to anyone seeking to understand the place of the medieval period with the wider history of Christian hostility to Jews.

The Origins of Racism in the West. Edited by Miriam Eliav-Feldon, Benjamin Isaac, and Joseph Ziegler. Cambridge: Cambridge University Press, 2009.

A wide-ranging collection of interesting chapters on the question of the historicity of using the term and concept of "race" in the medieval period. Although only one focuses on medieval Jews, the collection as a whole is extremely relevant to anyone interested in the debate over "medieval antisemitism."

The Trial of the Talmud. Edited by John Friedman, Jean Connell Hoff, and Robert Chazan. Toronto: Pontifical Institute of Mediaeval Studies, 2012.

A collection of Latin and Hebrew sources on the momentous thirteenth-century "trial" of the Talmud translated into English and preceded by a very useful introduction/essay by Robert Chazan.

Trachtenberg, Joshua. *The Devil and the Jews: The Medieval Conception of the Jew and its Relation to Modern Anti-Semitism*. Philadelphia: Jewish Publication Society, 1993.

This book is a classic, albeit slightly dated, pioneering work on the systematic demonization and dehumanization of Jews in medieval Europe. Originally published in 1943.

Vidal Doval, Rosa. *Misera Hispania: Jews and Conversos in Alonso de Espina's Fortalitium Fidei*. Oxford: Society for the Study of Medieval Languages and Literature, 2013.

A nicely readable and comprehensive analysis of the depiction of Jews and *conversos* in the notorious work of Alonso de Espina, the most vitriolic anti-Jewish propagandist of medieval Europe.